What readers are saying about
Building Your Dream Life

"...a true self-help book...clearly written, delightfully easy to read, highly focused, and positively empowering. The author offers down-to-earth, practical and attainable advice...of great value to high school graduates, college students and anyone who wants to learn more, to do more, to achieve more and to feel better about oneself." (Sacramento Public Library)

"...the only book that tells you HOW to be a success...a much-needed book that fills a void in available books." (Kathryn Favors, Ed.D.)

"...positive, powerful and packed with good ideas for success in life and in business." (Barbara A. Scott, Zenar Books)

Building Your Dream Life

Life planning and financial planning

©2008

Bobbie Christensen

Effective Living Publishing
Sacramento, CA

Published by Effective Living Publishing
PO Box 232233, Sacramento, CA 95823
(916) 422-8435 - ELPBooks@aol.com
www.BooksAmerica.com

Cover design Mustang Graphic Designers
www.MustangGFX.com
MustangGraphic@aol.com
(916) 422-7109

This publication is designed to provide accurate and authoritative information in regard to the subject matter covered. It is sold with the understanding that the publisher is not engaged in rendering legal, accounting, or other professional service.

ISBN: 978-0-9729173-8-4

Table of Contents

Introduction

I want to thank everyone who helped with this book particularly all of you who allowed me to use your real-life accomplishments as examples in this book. Some of the names have been changed and in some cases I have combined the stories of more than one person into just one individual to create more interest.

Many thanks to my husband of 27 years, Eric, for his continuing emotional support as well as the use of his talent for remembering what I have forgotten.

All of the information included in this book actually comes from our other books plus the previous 2nd edition of *Building Your Dream Life*. For more information on how to do some of these things, you will want to refer to our other books that cover those particular subjects in much more detail (see listing at end of book).

Finally, be aware that as with all my previous books, the purchase of this book comes with free consulting at any time. Just email me at ELPBooks@aol.com and include in the subject line "book".

Use this information that I and many others have learned to attain your own dream life.

Chapter One
Your Dream Life

It was a dark and stormy night with lightening and huge bangs of thunder when Susan laid her head on her kitchen table and sobbed her heart out. Her husband of ten years, Tom, had left a week ago for work and, after she had called the police several times when he did not come home that night, she received the divorce papers tonight when she had arrived home.

She had pretty much figured out that he must be having an affair although he kept denying it. She was angry because she now had two kids to support by herself but she had known it was only a matter of time. They had met, dated for two weeks and married without ever getting to know each other. Neither had been happy for a long time. They had to be the epitome of a couple having nothing in common. It was just through shear stubbornness on both their parts that the marriage had survived this long.

However, on top of handling this situation, she had been laid off from her secretarial job this morning. Susan had known the company was having financial problems. That was no surprise to her either as she had seen how top heavy the business had become in executives with no increase in support staff. Then the construction business had slowed down much more than it usually did in the winter so money was very slow coming in. And did the boss lay off any of the highly paid engineers? No, he just pared down the support staff even more saying he had to keep the professionals for when business improved.

Susan had to admit that under different circumstances she would have been pleased to have the opportunity to find a new job with friendly people and a boss who listened to her advice.

However, the final straw had come tonight when she opened up the mail to find a notice that the bank was foreclosing on her house, the home that she loved. Tom had always taken care of the finances and she knew he had a very good job making excellent money. Susan just didn't understand this until while trying to find Tom she had reached his mother who told her that he knew she would get the house so had not made the mortgage payments for over six months. Instead he had been using that money for a down payment on a new house for he and his new girlfriend. And he had put the new mortgage in the girlfriend's name so Susan would not be able to touch it.

This was the last straw. She couldn't even imagine leaving Texas. This she did not understand at all. 'What am I going to do?" she sobbed into her hands.

Charlie was worried. He loved working his family dairy farm. It was hard work but he had always found it very satisfying. Of course, he had not planned on inheriting it so soon but his father had died three years ago from a massive heart attack. His mother, Diane, was welcome to stay with Charlie and Denise and the three kids for as long as she wanted. Diane took care of the kids and meals while Denise worked a full-time job to help keep the farm going. But Charlie knew the odds of keeping a small family dairy farm running without throwing in with the big companies were very slight if not impossible.

They could probably get by for a few more years but would end up losing the farm to the bank. None of them wanted to sell out to a big company. And now their oldest son, Michael, was 15 years old and talking about going to college some day. Charlie didn't see how that would ever happen. Even if he sold the farm, where would his mother go? He wasn't trained for any other work and couldn't imagine working for someone else. And Denise. They had gone to school together since she had moved into town in third grade. They had been best friends and then lovers. They were married immediately out of high school planning to work the farm with his parents and raise their family there. Charlie knew that Denise wanted to be at home instead of in that office every day away from her family.

All he had was his very supportive wife, his kids, and 160 acres of farm land in Illinois. He might not have any savings or even health insurance, but Charlie knew he had to find a way to stay on the farm.

Helen had come from a working class family and knew the meaning of work. Work meant she could have more then her parents and brother and sister had. She could be comfortable, travel, have friends and someday marry the right person. And, since last year when her father had retired, she now knew that work meant she could retire and continue to live comfortably and not have to work till the day she died.

So Helen had attended college and spent the last 10

years doing what she loved most, teaching third graders about the world around them. She had a nice apartment and took a two week vacation each year traveling to some exotic location. She still hadn't found the right person to marry but was trying to be patient. And she was saving for her retirement at the age of 31 with her state employees pension plan at work. She was happy with her life.

Helen needed someone to make her life complete. However, she had already run through all of her friends single male acquaintances and didn't know where to look now. She needed to sit down and make a plan in order to get what she wanted in her life.

Susan and Charlie also needed their own plans. And, more importantly, plans that would bring them the kind of life they each wanted. It is always much better to make plans in a relaxed atmosphere rather than an emergency situation, however, it is never too late to make plans for a better life for you and your family.

There are two types of plans that cover two different time periods. There are the short term plans that cover what you want to accomplish in the next year of your life, kind of like New Years' Resolutions. This includes what you want to do this year, what you want to accomplish such as finding a new job that you actually enjoy, buying a new car instead of taking the bus everywhere, finding someone to love who will love you back. This is **SHORT TERM LIFE PLANNING.**

Some things you might want to accomplish do not

cost anything. Still, some things do take money to accomplish. And, of course, you still have to pay your bills every month. That means you also need to do **SHORT TERM FINANCIAL PLANNING**.

Then there are all those things you want to accomplish in life such as traveling, providing a college education for your children, buying your first home, getting into a great career or even starting your own business, and being able to retire comfortably. These are examples of **LONG TERM LIFE PLANNING**. Most of these things do require a great deal of money which brings you to **LONG TERM FINANCIAL PLANNING**.

Me, Inc.

In order to have the life you want, you need to think of it (that is, every aspect of your life) as a business. If you were president of Disney, you would need to create a five year plan to show your employees where you want to go and what you need to do to get there. Your life is your company so it also needs a plan. This will give you something firm to head for along with the necessary steps for getting there. 90% of all the businesses in this county are small businesses having less than five employees. Well, your company, Me, Inc., has less than five employees - - you and your immediate family of wife and children.

A large company like Disney has an accounting department and a research and development (R&D) department. You are a small company so you will be doing these things yourself. You will be creating the budget and planning how to buy the things you want. You are the one who will research all the options available to you and develop the plan for accomplishing those things.

Your future depends on how you handle Me, Inc. There are social scientists who believe that people are born with an instinct for either good or evil, for happiness or sadness. I certainly cannot disprove this and even think they are probably correct up to a point. That point is where each of you decides for yourself whether to do the right thing or the wrong thing, whether to do something to make your life happier or sadder. These are choices you must make and they require making changes in your life. For some people change is a wonderful challenge. For others, change can be very scary. It is much easier to leave things as they are. It is much harder to actually do what is necessary to create a change, if not physically harder, at least mentally more difficult.

Unfortunately, you have a lot of outside influence trying to run your company for you. If anyone, family or friend, is telling you to do or not do something that you really want to do, sit quietly and figure out why they are doing this. Are they truly afraid of you hurting yourself physically or failing in that attempt and hurting yourself emotionally? Or are they voicing their own fears?

Your parents dream of your being a surgeon even though you faint at the sight of blood. Your friends want you to be just like them, otherwise they might feel jealous of your accomplishments. If you find this happening to you, it is time to distance yourself from your family and make new friends. Maybe you just need to move to be a little further away from the family or maybe you need to move to the other side of the country. Meet new friends who are interested in the same things you are so you will have some emotional support.

**"The greatest pleasure in life
is doing what people say you cannot do."
Walter Bagehot**

Whether you find yourself in a relaxed atmosphere like Helen or in an emergency situation like Susan and Charlie, the first thing to do is make short term plans. Everyone must have a monthly budget to make sure the bills are paid and there is food on the table, but in order to enjoy your life you also need to plan beyond those basics to include the fun things in life. For Susan this will include finding another job or jobs (if Tom will not pay any child support) and paying the monthly bills. Once this emergency is taken care of, she can plan and create the life she wants to live both short term and long term. For Charlie short term planning means finding a way to make more money and cut costs so he can pay the monthly bills. After that he can start planning long term goals including his children's education. For Helen it means defining what is important to her so she can find another person that she can love for the rest of her life. This could take a short time or long but she will put include it under short term planning.

Helen, Susan and Charlie were lucky in that they had a mutual friend, Margie, who knew all about planning. In fact, she had learned about planning the hard way, by being forced to learn how to get organized and create her own plans to get what she wanted in life. And all three of these people were very glad that email had been invented!

Margie and Helen did not stay in contact much. They exchanged the usual Christmas letters but that was about it. Helen knew that Margie had a great marriage. But Helen also had a great deal of pride. She didn't stop to think that pride was one of the deadly sins for a reason - - it can ruin your life. So how could she contact Margie (out of the holiday season) without sounding needy and desperate? After tossing and turning all night with this problem constantly in mind, she awoke with a great solution. They might have lost contact with each other but there was still one very important thing they still had in common.

Chapter Two
Short Term Planning

Margie always checked her email first thing every morning. When you run a home business, this is very important. But she was surprised, no, make that amazed, to see an email from Helen. However, she was even more astounded at what Helen was asking her. They had been good friends in high school but Helen had gone on to college and Margie had gone out into the work world. From there on their lives seemed to just keep growing further and further apart. But they had both always loved to cook. In fact, they had spent a lot of evenings and weekends "creating" new recipes. Unfortunately, all this cooking had also created a weight problem for both of them. Margie had solved her problem with planned workouts every single day and changing her eating habits. The last she knew Helen still had the problem. And evidently she was not doing anything about it as Helen had emailed asking for their old recipe for Caramelized Pear Cake.

Considering how much they had loved this cake, it seemed very unusual that Helen had lost this recipe. In fact, she should have had it memorized by now. But Margie emailed it to her.

The next day she received another email from Helen asking about a tiny change to the recipe. Then she got another email. And another. The scope of information broadened also. She talked about her job and asked how Margie's business was doing. Finally she got around to the real reason for all of this correspondence. How did Margie find a great man that she had been happy with for so many years?

Now this last letter made sense to Margie. Helen seemed very happy with her life except for marriage. So Margie helped her put a plan together for finding the right mate.

There are some things in life that will last a lifetime yet are not long-term life plans because we need them and want them to happen much sooner then five years from now. You might be 20 years old and still enjoying your freedom and not be interested in settling down yet. Congratulations! You have figured out that marriage will not solve all of your problems. Or maybe you are 30 and wanting that place and person to come home to, someone you can know will be there for you. Or maybe you are 40 and very unhappy with the relationship you have. Maybe it's time for you to decide whether to change that person.

How do you interpret "change that person"? Do you think it means to change partners or are you thinking, "How do I get him/her to change so I can be in love again?"

First of all, we do not promote divorce. However, there are some things that we feel the only answer is divorce such as a person who has a drug or alcohol problem or any other disruptive or illegal addiction such as gambling. In this case, you cannot change that person. They have to want to change themselves and that may never happen. Then you need to seriously think about divorce and getting on with your life.

However, it seems like today people get divorced because they had an argument or he refuses to pick up after himself because his Mom always did it for him or she is spending too much money because she is lonely. These are situations where you love this person very much but feel like you just cannot put up with them any more. Many people say that you might as well give up because you cannot change anyone else (only yourself). However, one method that has worked very well for the last hundred years is to treat your loved one like a dog.

If you have a dog, you know that to train them to sit on command you have to reward them when they do it right and scold them with "bad dog" (in a stern voice) when they do something wrong. The same thing works with humans. Think of how you feel when you do something that takes extra time and someone tells you what a good job you did (smiling and saying, "Good dog," and patting him on the head). And think of how you feel when someone does not just tell you that you did something wrong but tells you how you screwed up again and you are hopeless. If you still love your spouse, smile and tell them when they do a good job and smile and tell them how it should have been done when they do something you do not like. This can save your relationship and does not even cost any thing.

There are a lot of theories concerning the #1 home wrecker. Some say the biggest problem is arguments about money. Some think being married to a workaholic will be nothing but problems. I think boredom is the #1 problem. If one of you are bored with your marriage, you tend to spend more time at work or anything else that will get you away from that situation.

How do you cure boredom in a marriage? I have seen couples who are just getting by financially but who spend all their free time together (kind of like when you were dating) and doing free things like hiking together, biking, swimming, even blackberry picking and they have as much fun as any millionaire. You do not need to be rich to have fun together.

If you are bored and end up sitting home with the kids during your spare time, think of thinks to do that the kids and you will enjoy. How about going fishing or playing an old-fashioned board game together (or play video games if they can be played as a family).

If you are bored with each other, what is there to look forward to. If you actively plan how to have fun together, whether it is fun sex, fun travel, or fun hobbies, you will have a happy marriage. The planning part is usually part of the enjoyment. As with all other aspects of your life, having nice things to look forward to will improve your life. Just like your career, your marriage needs planning and hard work to be successful. So sit down tonight with him/her and list some things you both want to do whether it is this weekend, next week, or next year.

However, maybe you are to the point that you want to find that special person. The good thing about finding that special someone is that it does not have to cost much and will fit into most budgets.

The first thing Helen needed to do was figure out what she wanted. This step can be compared to shopping for a new dress. Before you go shopping (if you want to save yourself a lot of time) you need to figure why you want the dress. To look sexy or to be comfortable hiking in. And to determine what will look good on you, you need to know what style is right for your figure and what colors to say nothing of what type of fabric do you prefer.

Therefore, the first thing Helen needed to do was create a list of what she liked, what made her comfortable, what made her happy, and what was important to her. None of this had anything to do with a mate, but rather what she needed and wanted in her life.

Of course, everyone's list will vary but it is important to WRITE this list down and keep the list.

"Humans are social animals who were meant to live in groups."
(Linda J. Bailey)

What did Helen like doing in her life? She liked the outdoors and hiking and swimming. But she also liked sitting home in the evening reading a good book. She liked sharing a meal with good friends. She certainly loved traveling. Teaching was very important to her. And kids were, too. She liked decorating her apartment in bright colors and usually wore bright colors also. She definitely liked good food (a little too much). Her family lived a long ways away and she lived very independently of them. However, the church she had been raised in was important to her. Now all Helen had to do was find a man who liked the same things.

However, just liking to do the same things is not the end of your list, it is just the beginning. You also need to add at the bottom of this list some finer detail to help you make a wise decision. What if any are your requirements for level of intelligence in this other person, what type of personality, or physical looks? Does he/she have a career that you can respect? What about some of the things that could eventually drive you crazy such as their level of cleanliness (this includes picking up after themselves). Too many people just assume that others are neat and clean only to find out when it is too late that that person is a slob. If you love having pets, what would happen if you ended up with someone who really does not want anything to do with animals (my Mother taught me that a man who does not like animals is not to be trusted and she was right). Does he/she have career plans that will mesh with your plans? Does that person want children or not, do their feelings concerning religion match your feelings?

It seems as though these things have nothing to do with love, but they do. It is one thing to fall madly and passionately in love and another thing to stay in love. This is why making this list is so important. In the rush of a new love it is easy to lose track of the criteria you have already set for yourself. When you think you are serious about someone, go home and check that list before you proceed any further. The next thing you do is meet their parents and friends.

Note that I said meet their friends and family rather

than yours. A persons family can tell a lot about that person. Let's say you meet his parents and find that his Mother is hovering over him. Is he going to expect the same treatment from you? Does her Dad tell her, in your presence, that he wants to buy her a new car? How spoiled is she and will you be able to live with that. The same thing goes for friends. Is he a wonderful sober person when you go out but a short visit with his buddies finds him continually drinking? Do you think she is the perfect person until you find out her girl friends talk about nothing but their latest purchase?

All of this does not mean that you have to wait for the perfect person. For one thing, the perfect person does not exist. But a person who meets most of the items on your list will make it easier to live with the items he did not quite live up to.

But first you have to meet someone or, preferably, a lot of someone's, so you have a choice.

Other then church, Helen really did not have much opportunity to meet anyone. And she did not like what she found at bars so how was she going to meet anyone? Online dating seems to be what a lot of people were doing. But what if she met someone who lived hundreds of miles away? She does not want to leave California!

In order to meet new people and make new friends (including men, preferably single) who liked the same things she did, she needed to get out there and find them. After all, even Cinderella had to make an effort to get to the ball to meet Prince Charming.

First, she let all of her friends and relatives know what she was looking for. She realized that she attended church every Sunday morning but, other than that, she was not really involved with church. She was amazed to find out that there was a single's group that met at the church every month and planned events together. Through that group she started another group who liked to travel and liked the outdoors but, figuring meeting just once a month was not going to help her, she volunteered to expand the group to weekly meetings with a trip once a month. Realizing that the church did not have that many singles to choose from, she volunteered to do advertising for the church to let the community know what they did.

But Helen needed to expand past just her church. With coaxing from Margie, Helen found that there were a lot of other places to meet people right in her own city. She found that there were actually two hiking groups in her city, however, both of them were for really advanced hikers. With Margie's encouragement she actually started her own hiking group for people who just liked to get out and walk. She just put a little ad in the paper, "New walking group for singles. Meet at Main St. library every Thursday at 6:00 pm or call 555-5555 for more information."

Helen began to realize that she had lots of interests that she had completely forgotten about. She had always loved theater and actually put on a play for the school and parents each year with her third graders. Now she decided to work as a volunteer usher at one of the local theaters. Because of her love of reading, Helen started a local singles reading group that met once a week at the bookstore.

What surprised Helen was that she enjoyed spending time with all of these groups and she was making new friends who enjoyed the same things she did.

But could she find the right man to spend the rest of her life with?

You will have your own list of things you love to do. Maybe you are like Helen and enjoy the simple things in life. Or maybe you enjoy skiing, snowboarding, sailing, surfing, decorating, woodworking, etc., things that are more expensive to pursue. Do not worry about the cost at this point. Shortly you will be planning your finances so that you can afford the more expensive pleasures. And, if you work on your budget and find you just do not have enough extra money for these expensive things, there are always the simple pleasures in life you can enjoy right now while saving for the more expensive ones.

Susan spent a long night of crying and thinking over and over again, 'What am I going to do?' But eventually she did fall asleep. She awoke to sunshine and actually smiled as she thought that at least she had got a lot of sleep because she didn't have a job to have to hurry to. But, as she sat up in bed rubbing her eyes, she realized she was still in a terrible mess.

Sometimes when we are in a difficult situation, a miracle happens. Well, this was not any miracle but

Margie happened to call Susan to see if she could come and visit her for a couple of days vacation.

"You are always welcome to visit but I'm afraid things are not going well here. You would have a much more pleasant vacation somewhere else."

"You know what I like about your problems," Margie asked? "I am really excited because they are YOUR problems and not mine," she laughed. "Seriously, I will be there tomorrow about noon and I promise we will solve your problems."

'Oh, sure," she thought. At least she would have a shoulder to actually cry on.

Margie arrived by taxi with a small suitcase and a very large pocketbook. Actually it looked like a cross between a pocketbook and a backpack. After a quick hug, Margie was all business. Sitting at the kitchen table, she pulled out a large lined notepad and a couple of pens as Susan got them each a large ice-cold Coke.

"We need to put your problems in order of importance," Margie began. So they created a list of all the problems with the most critical at the top. Finding a new job was first as Susan needed money coming in. Right along with that was talking to the bank and working out something so she would not lose the house as Susan really wanted to keep her home that she loved. She needed to have a heart-to-heart talk with Gene and Linda, 9 and 7 years old respectively. They needed to understand what had happened and why. Margie added "hobbies" to the list which surprised Susan.

"At a time like this, I don't think I have the time or money or energy for any hobbies!"

"This is when you DO need hobbies. You will need some time each day to do pleasant things and relax and even smile again," Margie explained. "So what do you love to do or would love to do if you had the time or money?"

The list of interests was long and Margie divided it into two lists. One was the list of things that were easy to do and cheap and could be done every week. She wanted to clean the house and throw out everything related to Tom. Forget about calling him to come pick up his things. Susan was just going to send them to the garbage. After that, she found it very difficult to think of things she liked to do. The last ten years had been filled with working, the children, and taking care of the house. Tom had hobbies like watching sports every weekend and playing pickup games with his friends. But she had nothing.

She didn't know if these would be considered hobbies, but she added cooking to the list (she loved cooking but never seemed to have the time) and thought she might like to try painting (she had actually won first prize in a high school art show). Margie added some other things to the list like going to church. She knew Susan had not attended in years but told her there would be others there going through the same things that she could talk with. In fact, Margie grabbed the phone book and in five minutes had found a church with volunteer counselors and made an appointment for Susan.

"What ever happened to your music?" Margie

asked.

"I can't afford a piano and, besides, I was never good at it."

"Being good is not necessary to having a hobby that you enjoy. Do you know anyone who has a piano?"

"Mom does but I don't know that she would give it to me. I know it's worth a lot."

But, with Margie's encouragement, Susan got on the phone and, after some hemming and hawing, asked her mother. Mom was happy Susan was interested in the piano again as it had always been her own love in life. In fact, under the circumstances, Mom agreed to hire a truck and get some strong friends to bring it over. "But remember, this is just a loan. That piano means a lot to me and I do want it back some day."

Susan's next list included long-term plans such as touring Europe and, in fact, touring America which she had never seen much of.

By this time Susan was smiling just from thinking about doing these things she enjoyed. Sometimes it is best to take a few minutes and think about the fun things you want to do before getting to the serious business of making a living. It will improve your mood which will help you think more clearly, particularly if you are in a crisis mode and need help fast.

**"The greatest discovery of my generation
is that human beings can alter their lives
by altering their attitude of mind."
William James, Psychologist**

So Susan spent some time thinking about the fun things, but now it was time to get down to the hard part.

"If you could do anything in the world every day, what would your very favorite thing be?" Margie asked.

People should be happy going to work each day. Now, stop laughing! You know that statement is true. Unfortunately, real life gets in the way of our pursuit of happiness. So be patient. We will talk about what you 'have' to do in a bit. For now, just follow this line of thought.

"I guess my favorite thing is cooking. I would love to be able to cook all day. And not just desserts but healthy low-cal stuff, too." Then Susan laughed. "Of course, I still would like to find my Prince Charming. But I suppose that will never happen," she sighed.
"Well, one thing at a time. Let's find you a job so you can pay the bills but something you love to do."

Susan had a lot of "buts" to add to that. But how could she make enough money to keep the house when she had no training as a professional cook? She was a trained secretary and she was good at it, but she did not like doing it.

The one thing that keeps people from accomplishing everything they have ever dreamed of is fear. Or maybe we should say Fear, with a capital F. Everyone needs a certain amount of fear as it protects us from doing some pretty stupid things in life. But is working for a living a stupid thing?

Although fear may be the number one deterrent, there are other things that stop us dead in our tracks also.

How many people are working in jobs because their parents, their teachers, and even their friends tell them how good they are at that particular thing. Keep in mind that Einstein couldn't pass math classes but became a famous physicist. Why, because that subject fascinated him to the point that, no matter what he was doing, he could not get it out of his mind. You know your parents always wanted what was best for you but too often parents are forcing their children to go to college when they are not cut out for it. Parents and teachers believe that the only way to get a good job (good means making more money) is to go to college or go back to college to retrain for something else.

**"Education is not an important factor
In amassing wealth."
Dr. Joyce Brothers**

**"Wealth is not an important factor
in amassing education."
Bobbie Christensen**

We all know that we are supposed to grow up some day. Unfortunately, too many people never do. After all, it is much easier to listen to your parents and friends and let them tell you what to do then it is to leap into the unknown on your own. You need to decide what type of person you are and what type you want to be (because you can change yourself if you really want to).

You may be the 'safety' type of person. This is someone who listens to others and does what is expected of them. Or you may be the 'risk taker' type of person. This is the one who realizes they are taking a risk but feel there is a good chance that the risk will pay off for them in a big way. If you are already the 'risk taker' kind, then you don't need to read this section. But if you are the 'safety' kind, *and* you would like to try being a risk taker, you need to retrain yourself.

First of all, the risk needs to be worthwhile or something that means a tremendous amount to you and that you truly feel will bring you happiness (and perhaps good fortunate). Second, you need to make a plan! Very seldom does something happen through pure luck or accident. Third, once you have made that plan, you need to learn how to grit your teeth and do it. Fourth, persistence pays off!

Attitude "is more important than facts...
more important than the past,
than education, than money...
than appearance, giftedness or skill."
Charles Swindoll

Actually creating a plan makes gritting your teeth much easier. If Susan loves cooking, how will she get there. First comes the plan.

A plan is actually a list. Well, Susan knows how to apply for a job so that is not a problem. Her concern was where would she find a cooking job and how could she seem to be qualified for it? But this is why humans are considered superior beings - - because we can reason things out!

This is where having a friend like Margie can really help. Sometimes people are so frightened of the unknown that they literally cannot think straight. Susan was terrified of losing her job and her house to the point where she could not think logically but could only think, 'what am I going to do.'

With Margie's help, Susan started a list of possible jobs. Fast-food cook at a restaurant really did not appeal to her as she didn't consider that really cooking. She did not have the training to work in a really good restaurant. She did have a lot of really good recipes and could perhaps put together a cook book.

"Okay," Margie smiled. "Writing a cook book is a great idea but it takes time and right now you need to find a job that involves your cooking to keep the wolf away from the door."

Susan was shocked. Her eyes went round and her mouth literally dropped open. How could she possibly work in a restaurant with no training?

"We just need to combine what you want to do with what you know how to do," Margie encouraged her.

Margie was actually Charlie's cousin. In fact, she had fond memories of summer vacations spent on the farm. Margie and her husband, Gary, still visited the farm a couple of days every summer. It was on the next trip that Margie found out she might not have a farm to visit next year.

The conversation between the cousins and good friends started out pleasantly with catching up on what everyone had been doing for the past year.

"I love visiting here in August and sitting out on the porch in the evening just like we did when we were kids."

"Yes," Charlie laughed, "But you didn't have to get up at 5:00 am to do the milking." She had to agree with that. "I guess I may not have to worry about that much longer either."

With gentle prodding from Margie, he slowly explained the situation. Denise and he as well as the kids loved the farm but he just could not see any way to keep going too much longer.

"Well, that seems like a simple enough problem," Margie stated in a matter of fact tone. "All you have to do is make more money."

Charlie didn't know whether to laugh at her or say something nasty. He did know that she obviously did not know what she was talking about. He started to open his mouth but Denise put her hands over his before he could say anything. Just that physical touch seemed to calm him down. He glanced over at Denise then back to Margie. He took a deep breath and quietly asked, "Do you have any ideas how we could do that?"

"Of course, I do," Margie smiled. "If a rich person like Bill Gates wants to make more money, how does he do it? He expands his business. You need to diversify into more things that will create more income for you. And," she quickly continued as Charlie leaned forward and looked like he was about to yell at her, "You need to do it with things you can do right here on the farm. After all, you have a lot of help. I know Denise would rather be working here than in an office to make more income and you have three healthy kids that can help, too. And you know Diane (Charlie's Mother) wants to keep the farm. You have everything you need right here!"

Neither Charlie or Denise looked convinced. Then, on top of all this foolishness, Margie wanted them to call the children in on this discussion.

"Oh, we don't want the children to worry," was their immediate reaction.

"But the children are not small. You have 15 year old Mike who wants to go to college so your family finances definitely concern him. Dickie may be only 13 years old but you said he wants to continue on the farm as his career. And what about Joan? She is the smartest of the lot and probably should also go to college. She needs to start saving for that now. And, if you expect her to help, than she should be involved, too. And I'm sure Charlie that your mother does not want you to lose the farm. She is strong and healthy and can help also."

"But they're just children. Joan is much to young to get involved. And Diane takes care of the kids when I'm at work"

"Then why not give Joan and Diane the choice as to whether to be involved or not?"

Everyone sat at the big kitchen table. Margie was thinking that it helped that it was a bright sunny day and the kitchen was warm and comfortable. In the middle of a dark dreary night is not the time to try to make major life decisions.

"Okay," Margie began, "The farm is having a financial problem. How many of you want to stay here on the farm?" The parents and two of the children raised their hands. "Okay, how many of you would rather move to a smaller house or an apartment?" No one raised a hand. "Joan, you didn't answer."

Joan had a very serious look on her face. "I want to stay here but we need to do what is best for the family. Mom and Dad always say that the family comes first. So I will go along with what is best."

Margie smiled. Joan was a great ally to have in this situation. "Well, I have some ideas that could bring in more money so you can keep the farm and that will be a lot of fun also."

First she suggested opening up the farm to guests and tourists.

"What?! Are you out of your mind? How can I run a dairy with strangers roaming around? And just think of the liability insurance I would have to pay."

But the rest of family picked up on the idea particularly little Joan.

> **"...the moment one commits oneself,**
> **then providence moves too.**
> **All sorts of things occur to help one**
> **that would never have otherwise occurred."**
> **Johann Wolfgang von Goethe**

Denise agreed that if they could get enough visitors to pay admission, she could stay home and take care of those visitors. Charlie could do his usual chores and she could take people on a tour of a real working dairy farm. Mother Diane agreed that she could help show them around the farm also. Although she couldn't walk a great ways, such as all the way down to the barn, she could show people the family garden and show how she preserved and canned all their winter food. Joan said they had to have a petting farm because whenever the "city" kids from school came to visit all they wanted to do was see the calves and kittens. Dickie felt that the farm was his life and because of that he already knew everything his father could possibly teach him so he could help with a lot of the day-to-day running of the farm. Everyone came up with a lot of ideas to make this a real working farm museum right down to Diane making her special pies and donuts for the visitors.

"But how can we get people to come here? Advertising costs a lot of money."

"Not if you know how to do it right, Charlie. First we need to focus on who we want to come here."

They all agreed that school trips would be great on Fridays when things were slower. And, living in Illinois, they knew they wouldn't have many people coming in the winter but the schools still had trips year round. Adults and families would come on weekends and summer would have lots of people traveling and visiting.

**"Life is either a daring adventure,
or nothing."
Helen Keller**

Everyone was now getting excited about the plans. Even Charlie was thinking this might possibly work. "Alright. Now we need to plan out every little detail. Denise and Diane will be in charge of that. I want to see lists of everything from hours of operation including seasonal dates to admission. Charlie and Dickie will be in charge of writing out exactly what each tour will include. That means a tour of the barn and milking operation, the equipment, and Dickie, get on the computer and dig up some interesting facts about farming like how much corn you produce per acre now compared with what your grandfather produced 30 years ago. Joan and Michael will work on where to put the petting zoo and how to operate it. And Michael will be in charge of the bookkeeping.

"But I don't like numbers!" he wailed. "I want to be an architect."

"Well, you have to understand numbers to be an architect and, if you ever want to run your own architecture company, you will need to understand the bookkeeping so no one cheats you. You don't want some unscrupulous employee stealing your money, do you?" Margie had known Mike the longest of the kids and understood him very well as well as what really mattered to him.

"Besides that, Mike, you will need to know how to advertise your company so you are in charge of advertising and Denise can help you with that."

"But we don't have the money to advertise," Charlie insisted.

"But you love what you do and you know how to tell people about it. You and Mike and I will sit down tomorrow to start work on the advertising. We have to have everything else in place first so we can provide operating hours and cost and such."

There was one thing that Margie had learned at a very young age with her friends. That it is always easier to solve other people's problems than her own. Why? Because you are too caught up in your own problems to think clearly. Sometimes having an outside person can really help. Think of it as having a clear head to help you. The problem, however, is finding someone to help you.

That is, he or she must be an optimistic positive thinker. Anyone else could tear you down and just make the whole situation worse then it already is. So this could be a friend, a relative, a teacher, your church minister, or someone you know but who you are not close to. The only criteria is that they must not have any hidden agenda.

Unfortunately, relatives and friends often do have

preconceived notions about you or may subconsciously not want you to succeed. Teenagers have a big problem with this because they have friends who tell them they are stupid or not pretty enough or whatever. What that friend is actually saying is, "I don't want you to become better then I am." Teachers should be unprejudiced but they are not. They also have preconceived notions of what you are like, what you are capable of, what you should do. So perhaps finding the right person to help you plan your life may be the most difficult thing to do.

However, keep in mind that if you can get your emotions under control and think in a clear-headed way, you can do all of this planning without any outside help, too.

The Importance of Lists

The second most important thing is not difficult at all but most people do not do it. That is, you must write everything down. Lists! You probably do this already but unfortunately you do it mentally. You daydream about what you would like to do but you never actually create a list and you end up forgetting some very important things. Dreams are what you create in your mind, life is what you create on paper first.

Although it would seem like money, as in paying the bills, financial planning should be the first thing to think about, you must start with planning your life both short-term as in what to do this week and this month to long-term including everything you have ever dreamed of accomplishing. Why? Because you will not know what your budget should look like unless you first know what you want to do. You cannot create a financial plan unless you know what it will need to cover.

Thus Susan sat down and created two lists. One included all the things she loved doing and the other contained all the things she had ever dreamt of doing some day. So she had a short-term list that included things like finding a new job and a long-term list of what she wanted to do with the rest of her life. Now she has goals to work toward.

Charlie and his family had several lists. Margie did not get them into their personal dreams yet because the family first had to save the farm which was their income as well as their love. But they had a lot of lists to cover a lot of business decisions.

That evening, everyone got busy planning and creating lists. They had lists of hours of operation and what they would charge that would eventually expand to include what time they would offer hay rides and when the petting zoo would be available. They also had a listing of what the farm tour would include and another list of what the "house" tour would include such as the garden and canning and preserving food. And they would create a list, including a calendar, of what they would do for advertising.

Charlie's family had a lot of lists because they were starting a business. Helen had a simple list: find someone to love that would love her in the same way.

Having dreams is what makes life bearable.

Without dreams you are only surviving. But just having dreams can become old after awhile. Sitting down and writing all these down on paper means you can now start working toward those dreams.

And don't lose these lists - - ever!

You do not want a list to look at once a year and just dream about. You want a list of what you want to do and how are you going to accomplish it. Then, as you do accomplish each step toward that dream, you can actually cross it off and see the list getting shorter and shorter and your dreams getting closer and closer.

Helen knew what she wanted but how was she going to find that person? She created her own personalized plan for meeting new people (including men). But again, it is easy to *say* you are going to do something but it takes some effort to actually create a plan. You can brain-storm for hours about how to get where you want to be but, without the plan, they are just dreams.

"Nothing can take the place of persistence.
Talent will not;
the world is full of unsuccessful people with talent.
Genius will not;
unrewarded genius is almost a proverb.
Education alone will not;
the world is full of educated derelicts.
Persistence and determination alone are omnipotent."
Calvin Coolidge

"...persistence overshadows even talent..."
Deepak Chopra

Helen spent several hours with Margie talking about all the organizations through the church as well as other public groups she could join and they talked about the groups Helen could start herself. When you spend some good time thinking about all these great things, you will feel energized and excited. You feel like you can get whatever you want in life. But then you go to bed. The next morning you again feel the excitement but you can't quite remember what those plans were. You remember something about checking out any groups the church might have but what was that other thing?

This is why lists are so important. Create the list of what you want to do in the coming year and what you want to do with the rest of your life. Then create a list for each of the items on the previous lists. Writing down that you want to "find a new job" is not a plan, it is just an idea. You then need to create a plan of how to get that new job. But what job? You may hate the job you are in but you need to know what you are looking for. We call it "what do you want to be when you grow up?"

Chapter 3
What Do You Want To Be When You Grow Up?

"**Some Common Myths About Money -**
Education will cause wealth. **This myth contends that a good education will ensure financial success. Millions of educated unemployed people would beg to disagree...*You must work very hard at a boring, awful job in order to make a lot of money.* It is this myth that makes us feel it is impossible to make good money by doing something we enjoy...if you do something you don't enjoy for work, it is almost guaranteed you won't get rich from it...Let loose of the idea that there is only one way to make money.**"
Linda J. Bailey, author of How To Get Going When You Can Barely Get Out of Bed

Everyone is asked from the time they are quite young, "What do you want to be when you grow up?" But now you need to get serious about it. You can just float from one job to another to make a living but that is not going to buy you a home of your own or provide for a family very well or pay for the things that you would like to do with your life.

The other problem is that people limit themselves. You might have been told by a teacher how good you were in math and, therefore, you became an engineer but find you really don't like the job. Or maybe you are still in school and studying law because your father was a lawyer and that is what your parents are paying the college for.

You must take charge of your own life. Yes, you

can certainly ask others you know what their opinion is but, in the end, you have to decide for yourself or look forward to years of unhappiness. So how do you figure out what you really want to be? Open up your mind to all the possibilities out there. Go to the library.

Now, we realize this sounds old-fashioned but, to decide what we want to do, the library is the easiest way. Yes, there are books (even on-line resources) that list all of the careers in the world - supposedly. To really get a clear picture though, go to the library.

They have a great system in that all books related to a particular subject are kept together. Take a pad of paper and pencil with you. Starting with the first shelf of books numbered 100 (the Dewey Decimal System), you will scan the titles of the books. This will also mean you need to grab one of their little step-stools to get to the very top shelves and to sit on for the bottom shelves. Go through one category at a time looking for any titles that interest you. Write down anything that you like whether it sounds too far fetched or not. For instance, maybe you are 50 years old but always wanted to be a ballerina. Well, it may too late to become a ballerina, but put it on your list anyway as it will be useful to you in the next step. If you come to roller-blading and love doing that, put it on your list. In other words, do not limit yourself to the usual recommended lists of careers. Just limit yourself to things you are very interested in or think you would really enjoy.

This really does not take as long as it sounds because you are not reading every single book title. You will skim the titles looking for areas of interest.

When your list is complete (you have scanned all the categories in the library), you need to start putting them in order with the things that sound the most interesting or fun at the beginning. Then take the first three to five items and go back to the library and take out two books on each of those subjects. Some of the items on your list you may already know about and do not need to read up on but others you will need to do a little more research to see how interesting they really are. You might love to play billiards and realize you could spend more time practicing and become good enough to enter tournaments. But these tournaments are all over the country and you really do not like to travel. Then you need to cross billiards off your list. This doesn't mean you can't still enjoy it as a hobby but it does not fit your criteria for a job (not traveling).

This research will pay off in the end when you find yourself making a career of something that you really love to do. You will actually be excited getting up at 6:00 am to go to work. But how do you turn billiards (or anything else) into a career? How can Susan take her limited knowledge and create a career in cooking? We will get to that shortly.

Today you need to concentrate on creating a plan of what you want to do or accomplish within the coming year.
Then you will create a plan(s) to accomplish these things.
Next you will start implementing those plans.
But the immediate future is most important as it will affect your long-range plans also. So what lists do you need to create?

Creating Your Own Lists

It is fine to talk about planning your life and creating lists but we realize that some people need a little more guidance in this area so let's use some actual examples.

Susan has some immediate problems that need to be solved quickly. She needs to keep her house and find a new job. Keep in mind that short-term life planning means what you want to accomplish within the coming year. Obviously Susan cannot afford to take a whole year to find a job but it falls within that one year period. There are other things that need to be on the yearly list also. Everyone needs something to look forward to. So here is Susan's short-term life planning list:

> Talk to bank about house mortgage
> Find new job - Cooking
> Practice piano in time for Christmas carols
> Try painting
> Travel

Note that the list is not huge and that your list could be very different. For instance, Charlie's list is:

> Make more money to keep farm
> > Create farm museum
> Save for kids education
> Continue working farm (because that is what he loves to do)

Obviously Charlie is not all by himself. He has a family. Therefore, each member of that family also needed to create their own list and here is what they did.

Denise (his wife)
>Work at home
>More family time together
>More time for crafts
>More time for gardening

Diane (his mother)
>Keep the family farm
>More time for cooking like home-made taffy

Mike (his oldest son, 15 years old)
>Become an architect
>Save for college
>More time for woodworking and building

Dickie (his second son, 13 years old)
>Keep farm
>Spend more time working on farm equipment

Joan (his daughter, 11 years old)
>Have more pets

This is not to say that everyone in your family will want to plan for the future. A person needs to get to that point in life where the future becomes important and there is no way to force anyone to get to that point. Some people are almost born planning for the future. Others may not reach that point until they get married or start a family. And some people may never get to that point even though they need to. But keep in mind that those people will probably never accomplish the things they want to and it is a very sad situation to have reached the end of your life and have to say, "I wish I had done such-and-such."

"Oh, God, to reach the point of death
only to realize you have never lived."
Henry David Thoreau

As everyone is so very different, each of your lists will vary not just in what you want in life but also in how many things you really want to accomplish. None of Charlie's family had a long list. Helen has a longer list than she had planned on. She thought she had everything and just wanted to have her own family (starting with a husband) but soon realized that there was a lot more she could accomplish also. So here is her list.

Find the right man
Buy a house
Lose 60 pounds
Go hiking more
Travel more
More time to read
Get involved with theater and acting
Learn to: kayak, canoe, snow ski, water ski, etc.
Gardening?? Photography??

At this point in her life, Helen has a good career that she enjoys so there is nothing on her list about that. But lists should and do change!

These lists need to be hung up where you can see

them every single day. Keeping your goals constantly in front of you will help you achieve them. They will also keep your brain active thinking of new things to add to the list as well as other ways to achieve those things.

But suppose Helen tries gardening and does not like it? Then she can just scribble through that line. Don't erase it though. If you erase it, it is as though it never existed. By crossing it out you indicate that here is something you wanted to try and you did try it. Just trying new things is an accomplishment also.

And you can add to your list any time you want to. Your interests and ideals will change and it is okay to change your list also. After all, it is your life and that means you can do anything you want to.

But how do you get there? By planning the details.

Now it is time to create individual lists of how to get each of the things you listed. So how can Susan suddenly get not only a new job but a job that involves cooking? She has no experience in it (other than cooking for herself and friends) and no training in it. And she does not have time to go back to school. She needs a job now.

Finding Work You Love

Everyone is good at something and some of you are good at several things. But no one is perfect! That is, you may really enjoy doing something that you are good at but not great at. You could love playing the trumpet but you are never going to be great at it. That does not mean you cannot still make a living doing what you love, you just have to think about going through the back door. Instead of trying to make a living in a band, how about teaching trumpet to students and any adults that might be interested? You may never be a great painter, but you can still teach painting or create murals for store windows. You may love skateboarding so how about teaching other kids how to do it and even starting local or even statewide championships in the sport. If you just want to fly kites all day, start evening and weekend classes on building kites and taking these classes outside to actually fly them. If you love to travel, you can set up weekend trips for others who love to travel and you charge what the trip will cost plus your profit. Believe me, you can make a living at anything! And it is much easier to be successful at something you love to do rather than try to be successful at something just to make a living.

Susan loved cooking. She had some dishes she was great at. But she could not make a pie crust no matter what she tried. Other then working as a waitress while in high school, she had no professional cooking experience. Some people might say, "Then forget it or go back to school!"

But Susan does not have the time to go back to school, she needs a job now. Besides, she actually already has the knowledge, she just does not have the credentials. Or she thinks she does not. Susan just needs to think about how to get where she wants to be by going through the back door. This gives her a huge range of possibilities. She has worked in business offices for years and has learned about managing a business through this work. She could apply to be a business manager at a restaurant. That would pay the bills but not be cooking. As going to cooking school is out of the question financially (besides which she really does not want to go to school again), Margie suggests looking for a restaurant manager's position to pay the bills while starting her own business in cooking.

However, just for a few minutes, let's say that Susan does not even have this business management background to use on her resume. You know that what an employer is looking for is someone who knows how to do the job. They actually look at educational background (as in college) assuming that the education has taught them how to do the job. The reality is that school very seldom actually teaches you how to do a job. You need real hands-on experience also.

When applying for a particular position you will need to show your knowledge (education) and experience. Keep in mind that knowledge is very easy and costs nothing. You need to become an expert in your new field.

"Everybody is learning just one thing,
not because they will know more,
but because they have been taught that
they won't have to work if they are educated."
Will Rogers

This is again where the library as well as your computer can help you tremendously. If you need to be able to put something under "education" that is related to the field you want, then take a class in it. No, I do not mean go to school necessarily. If you did take a class, what would be involved? You would have a teacher who would lecture, give you reading assignments and, hopefully, answer your questions. You can get all of this without paying tuition.

Get a catalog of required courses from your favorite college or university and find out what courses are required for the field you want to go into. Then contact the teacher of that class to find out what the required reading list is. You can get those same books through your public library (remember that they have lending programs so that if they do not have the book you want, they can still get it for you). Once you have finished those books and understand them, you can put on your resume:
  3 hours in Advanced Biology
  6 hours in Accounting
  3 hours in Business Law
The hours coincide with the credit hours you would receive if you attended the class.

Start reading magazines and periodicals concerning the field you want to go into. If your town has a college nearby, chances are they offer classes right on your TV. This is an easy way to learn more. Go to museums connected with your field. Attend lectures. And be sure to keep a written record of all these things you do.

Start a correspondence with a noted expert in your field. After reading a few books, you might have some questions. Susan did not understand a couple of examples her reading gave her but she could contact a local chef (maybe even at a restaurant she would like to work at) to ask him to clarify these questions. Keep up the correspondence so that some day you can use this person as a reference.

Have business cards printed even if you have not actually done anything in your business yet. If you have the opportunity to meet someone in the field, you need to convince them that you are serious about this business. Find a local support group for the area you want to go into or create your own. If Susan wants to specialize in cakes for all occasions, she could start a support group called "catering entrepreneurs" for others in the area who want to start their own catering service. Maybe another member specializes in weddings and can subcontract the cakes out to you. Or another does part-time work as a clown at children's parties but can recommend you for creating the cake.

"Imagination is more important
than knowledge."
Albert Einstein

You will also need to show experience on your resume. But remember that a lot of experience is transferable from one job to another.

"Most of our work is skilled and requires
Practice, and not education."
Will Rogers

Have you or can you volunteer? For instance, Susan has volunteered many times to create cakes for her friends special events. Because they were friends, she did not charge them. But on her resume she does not have to say that she did not receive any pay for these. All she has to list is that she has created cakes for anniversaries, weddings, etc.

And what about her idea to teach classes on cooking with herbs? Keep in mind that any speaking (teaching classes) or writing (a booklet for attendees) is part of your experience also. Let's say you have a gift for foreign languages. You can learn a new language just by listening to tapes and practicing. But because you do not have a diploma, you cannot find a teaching position for any foreign language. However, you also know that financially strapped schools are cutting out things like languages but a lot of parents still want their children to have knowledge of a foreign language. You could start your own tutoring classes for these kids.

"The creative thinker is constantly challenging the rules."
Roger von Oech

Even with all of this, you will still need to market yourself and your business. You need to know how to sell yourself to a potential employer. You do this through a resume. However, if you want to start your own business, you need to market that business in order to make a living. The best way to demonstrate marketing is to give you actual examples.

Charlie need's to let people know about his Farm Museum. So the family creates news releases for newspapers that will teach the reader's something interesting. For instance, maybe it is Fall and Diane does a short article on how to freeze fruit for the winter. Of course she cannot give all the necessary information in a short article but she can include a final paragraph saying, "For more information, contact Diane at The Farm Museum, 555-5555, 36 Long Meadow Road in Gilroy". Denise and Joan create flyers to send to the news director of radio and TV stations telling about how to take care of a pet duck (or cat or chicken or goat) and will mention their Farm Museum during the interview.

A plumber can promote his business by mailing news releases and offering media interviews on what to do if you suddenly find water all over the floor and, during the interview, offering his phone number for more help. The same marketing applies to any business you might start.

"The secret of success is
making your vocation your vacation."
Mark Twain

Although Susan had years of experience in business management, she decided to read some books specifically on restaurant management.

Susan could also start a part-time catering business perhaps specializing in children's parties. Although she cannot seem to master pie making, Susan is great when it comes to cakes so she could specialize in cakes for all occasions. Neither of these is expensive to start as it is a matter of getting your business in the yellow pages and then slowly building up your reputation.

Susan also loves cooking with fresh herbs. Perhaps she could teach cooking classes in her home. She could even teach people how to grow their own herbs using her patio garden as an example. She makes wonderful jams and jellies. This is a very competitive business but might be a possibility. Or she could work seasonally creating holiday dinners to order (just tell her how many people will be at your house for Thanksgiving and she provides everything). The list of possibilities for part-time businesses goes on and on.

However, Susan's favorite ideas are specializing in cakes and cooking with herbs. The problem is, it takes time to start your own business and she has a home to save and two small children to take care of. Therefore, earning a living comes first, but she can work on her own business part-time.

Susan lives outside of Austin but within an easy commuting distance so she starts by checking the Sunday paper for openings and goes online to look for any local openings. As there are not too many listings, she goes to her yellow pages and checks off every restaurant she could possibly work for. She will personally go to each of these places and try to talk to someone there about a job and make sure she leaves them her resume. Oh, oh! A resume.

There are a lot of different resume styles, all of which work quite well. The problem is not creating a professional looking resume, the problem is what to put in for experience. Think about what you have ever done in your life. Susan has cooked family dinners for years that included up to 20 family members. Then she remembered the family reunion three years ago that she had done virtually all of the planning as well as the cooking by herself. And her large extended family was always asking her to do birthday cakes and parties for them. On her resume, this experience became:

Experience:
Planned family reunions for several families including menu planning, location reservation, decorating, seating, hiring service help, etc.

Created custom birthday parties for children as well as adults including creating decorations, creating specialized cakes, buying all supplies through local wholesaler.

Susan had also taken a couple of business courses when she first started doing secretarial work. These became: Education - 15 credit hours including business management, business accounting, business law.

In other words, use anything you can, without lying, that shows what you are capable of doing.

After pounding the streets going to every restaurant there is, Susan landed a management position at a nice family style place in just one week. Yes, she spent 14 hour days looking for that job, but it paid off. But she had another problem. The job did not pay enough for her to live on. It would cover groceries, basic bills and part of the mortgage, but not everything.

But, with Margie's encouragement, Susan realized that she could also start her own business part-time for additional income. The quickest and easiest thing was to start herbal cooking classes in her home advertising through the local schools and colleges community education programs. Then Susan thought that if that class would only take up an average of four evenings a month, she still had time to also teach cake decorating which might also bring in some cake orders for her. And, when Spring came, she could teach classes on growing herbs using her own garden.

With all of this, there would not be much left for anything extra but Susan would be able to get by. Meanwhile, she owed six months of mortgage payments if she was going to keep her house. And how could she afford health insurance for the kids? And what about all the other things she dreamed of doing some day?

Susan had had fun creating her short-term life plan of finding a job and maybe even starting her own business but what about raising her kids with all the things they needed or ever being able to travel? Susan needed a financial plan and fast.

Chapter 4
Short-term Financial Planning

Susan had a big short-term financial problem. Thanks to her soon-to-be ex-husband, she was months behind in her mortgage and had received the first foreclosure notice.

It is a natural instinct to panic at times like this but panic will not solve a problem (unless you see a snake and panic and start to run). But this is also the most difficult time to think things through logically. What we suggest is when that feeling of panic is there, put a mantra into your head and think over and over again, "I must do step one, I must do step one."

Step one for Susan was to call the bank to make an appointment with someone in mortgage lending. This brings up another good point.

Keep in mind that if a reputable bank will not lend you the money to buy a house, chances are you should not have a house. That is, they check to see how much you make and how much you owe and make a logical decision as to whether you can afford a house or not. If the bank turns you down, do not go to a mortgage lending company. These companies were created quite recently due to Congress opening up the banking laws. However, they cannot compete with regular banks so they go after those people that really cannot afford to buy a home and, in the process, charge ridiculous amounts on unsafe loans. They know you will probably have a problem paying back that loan but, before you actually default, they can make a lot of interest off of you. You have seen this recently with the so-called "sub-prime" loans.

Susan went to her bank. She had taken the time to write up a list of the points the bank would need to know about, gave a copy to her banker, and then went through each point. She explained how her husband had taken the money but told her he was paying the mortgage, how she had just lost her job, went through her previous job history so he could see that she always worked and could find another job quickly, what she was doing to find a job, her plans for teaching classes and then what she proposed. She explained that she needed two months without another payment in order to find another job and get the money flowing again and then wanted to refinance the house in her name only. Keep in mind that unless you have a fantastic house and owe very little on it, the bank does not want to foreclose because it is going to cost them to do the foreclosure and sell the house for whatever they can get for it. Of course, if you have a fantastic house that is worth a lot but has less than its value still owing on the mortgage, the banker may see a chance for his sister to buy a great house at a very low price. Yes, this does happen.

The bank did not want Susan's house and were willing to work with her on this. They saw a sensible person who was in a bad situation but was going to make it right. The banker excused himself for a few minutes to go check out Susan's credit history. He could see that she had a steady work history and, other than the mortgage payment, everything else was always paid on time. She got the extension.

If you were in a different situation wherein even with a new job you would not be able to make the house payments, then think logically. If you cannot afford that house, it is time to sell it and get into a smaller house or an apartment that you can afford. Trying to make those monthly payments that you really cannot afford is just going to make your life miserable.

It's one thing to want something and another thing to actually get it. However, it is always much easier to attain those things if you have a plan. In the previous chapters we talked about one type of planning called short-term life planning. That is, what do you want to accomplish within the coming year of your life. Some of the more obvious things that we did not list were happiness, less stress, or having more fun because these things are usually free or cost very little. But even enjoying the outdoors costs something. Maybe you need to drive to a park and that costs gas money. Or you want to go for a hike but it is fall and you need a heavy coat for the weather.

And some short term items cost a lot such as paying the bills. But, again, even paying the bills is easier and less stressful if you have a plan for doing that. Every single person who receives money needs a short-term financial plan and there are no excuses. You cannot say it is too difficult because it is very easy to do. You cannot say you do not have the time because the collection agency is not going to care how much time you have. You cannot say you do not have enough money because that is the whole point, to make sure you do have the money to pay the bills. Interestingly, I just saw an ad on TV telling people how important it was to do financial planning but also saying how difficult and time consuming it is to do so let them do it for you. Talk about false advertising! All you need is a piece of paper, a pencil and enough fingers to add on (or a calculator).

Your Monthly Budget

Either create your budget on your computer so that you can just print out a copy each month or hand write it and make copies at work if you have to but, it must be written down.

It is impossible to include every bill you have because most people have an unusual bill that does not apply to most of you. Any unusual bills you have or one-time-only bills will be written in at the bottom each month. What needs to be on every budget? Let's use Susan's monthly budget for an example of what will be on yours. You will be using an average amount that you pay each month on each bill. If you do not know what the average is, then go through your last six months of bills for each item, add them up, and then divide by 6 to get an average amount.

Monthly Budget:

Mortgage/Rental	960.
Maintenance allowance	10.
Car payments	350.
Gas/Oil/Maintenance	240.
Other transp (taxi, bus, subway)	0.
Taxes (property, etc.)	80.
Utilities (electric, water, sewage, etc.)	120.

Groceries				1200.
Insurance				
Health				120.
Car				80.
House				80.
Credit Cards (4)	25.	65.	130.	90.
Loan payments				0
Clothing				10.
Recreation/Entertainment				20.
Charity				10.
Savings/Investments				10.

Mortgage

Susan has a mortgage and desperately wants to keep her house. But should she? If she really didn't care about the house or perhaps it holds bad memories for her because of the divorce, then selling it and moving into a more affordable apartment would not be an issue. But Susan really wants to keep this house so she lists the actual mortgage payment she has each month.

Although you want to live comfortably, you need to look at the issue of whether to rent or buy from a business point of view. That is, which makes more sense financially. If you are young and just starting out, you probably don't want to be tied down to one place as you may have to move for your career or you could meet someone you want to spend you life with but they live a thousand miles away.

However, if you marry and have the desire to settle down in one place, buying a house (in this case a home) makes sense *if you can afford it*. It seems to have always been the American dream to own your own home but should it be?

Again, this is where your monthly budget is going to help you. When everything is added up, what can you afford. Or, as in Susan's case, does owning a home mean so much to you that you are willing to sacrifice for it? For this example, we will include Susan's mortgage payment.

Car Payments and Other

Your monthly car payment or payments is pretty obvious but what about the "other"? Most people think about how much they have to pay for gas but have you added it up to see what your monthly total is? Susan guessed that she was using about two tanks of gas a week (she has only the one car). However, this is a number that can change from week to week. One week you could use one tank and another week you go to visit your sister or do a lot of holiday shopping and use three tanks. For now put down a reasonable amount that you think you spend on gas and then keep track of it. Buy a little notebook to keep in the car and each time you fill up the gas tank just list the date and the dollar amount.

If you want to learn something interesting, also put down the mileage and the gallons of gas each time. Then you can divide the number of miles since your last fill-up by the number of gallons to see how many miles per gallon you are getting. If you are getting 30 or more miles per gallon, that is good. If your mileage is considerably less, do you want to think about buying a smaller car that gets better gas mileage. And please be aware that what the car manufacturer advertises as the mileage and what your actual mileage will be are two different things.

What most people forget to add into this amount is how much you spend on maintenance and oil changes. Experts will tell you that the most important thing you can do to keep your car running for a long time is to change the oil according to the miles in your handbook. If you have an older car, plan on changing it every 3,000 to 4,000 miles.

What just about everyone forgets to add into this amount is other maintenance such as new tires, window wipers, tune up, etc. So add a few extra dollars to cover those things also.

As with the home versus apartment argument, you should also think about your car in the same way. If you are young with no one but yourself to support and you want to pay for an expensive sports car (and the high insurance that goes along with it), then that is your choice. Or you might be older and your children have already left home so you decide to spend the money you are saving on a sports car. But if you are married and have a family, you need to be logical. Again, both automobile experts and financial experts will tell you that it is better to buy a new car, keep it in good condition, and run it for 200,000 miles (or until it dies) then it is to keep trading every few years. Just doing this one thing can save you thousands of dollars over a ten year period.

Let's say you bought a new car and needed to make payments of $390 a month for 5 years. If you keep that car running for 10 years, after you have made the final payment in year 5, you will save $23,400 over the next 5 years of no monthly payments. Of course, you will need more repairs during that time but, even so, you will still save thousands of dollars.

Taxes

This includes your property taxes unless it is already escrowed into your mortgage payment and setting aside money to pay any other local taxes, county taxes, or state and federal income taxes above what has been taken out of your pay check. If you figure up your income taxes on April 15th and find that you owe $3,000, do you really want to go into more debt by using a credit card or loan to pay those taxes? That is certainly not the way to do it. Set aside a little each month for taxes. The worst that can happen is that you did not set aside enough but at least then you will not have to borrow as much. The best that can happen is that you do not owe any taxes and now you are due a refund to put into a nice little nest egg.

If you want to save on your taxes (aside from starting your own business), check and see if your property taxes are escrowed into your mortgage payment. For instance, Susan found that in the 10 years she and her husband had owned the house they had built up enough equity (value) in it that she was not required to escrow the taxes any more. That means she could get a reduced monthly mortgage payment if the lender approves it. Also, if her equity has built up enough, she does not need to pay the mortgage insurance included with her monthly payment (this is required by the lender until enough equity has been built up). If she qualifies, this insurance can be dropped saving her another $25 to $30 each month. However, keep in mind that the bank does not notify you about this. You need to contact the bank to find out if you now qualify for these reductions.

Utilities

Usually you can just take the same amount you paid last month and it should be pretty close. However, for some people the utilities can vary tremendously from one month to another. If you live up north, you may not have or need air conditioning in the summer but you will spend a lot more in the winter months for heating. If you live in the south you may spend a lot more on your air conditioning and water bill in the summer then you do in the winter. Because of these variations, you need to think of an average between the two extremes.

Groceries

Susan had never kept track of what she paid on groceries although she knew it was a lot more than her budget liked. Therefore, she decided to "guess" at about $400 a week or $1200 a month. As most people do not keep their grocery receipts, you may also have to "guess" for the first monthly budget. However, you will quickly learn whether you have guessed wisely or not.

It is strongly suggested that you take your grocery amount in cash out of your checking account and put that cash into an envelope marked groceries for three reasons. First, you will see very quickly if you have allowed enough for groceries. Second, too many people are charging their groceries. Third, this will establish a good way to review your grocery budget and see if maybe you can trim it down by eliminating the two cases of soda each month. We will talk about charge cards shortly but you should never charge groceries unless you are literally starving to death!

Because most people do not realize how much they are spending on groceries, they under-budget for this. Once you start keeping track of what you are spending, you will probably need to change this monthly amount and you will be able to see more clearly how you can cut back on the things you do not need.

Insurance - Health, Car, House

For now all you need to do is add up what you are

spending on each of these per month and put it on your budget. Later we will talk about which of these you really need to have and which ones you do not need or can handle in a better way.

Credit Cards

Americans have the largest amount of debt ever in history. Debt is a two-edged sword. Over the years credit cards have allowed people to spend much more money then they actually have which has contributed to our having a good economy. That is, the more money you spend, the more jobs there are out there, the more money those workers have to spend, creating more jobs, etc. So charge cards are great for our economy.

But for you as an individual, debt is usually not a good thing. There is good debt. For instance, for most people a home mortgage is the only tax deduction they have so it can be good for them to owe that money. But owing too much money means that when the bad times come (and they always do), how will you pay all that money back? You can buy anything you want with your credit card and pay just a small amount back each month. So long as you have a good job that covers all those bills, you are happy. But what happens when we go into a recession and you lose your job or your hours are cut back? Then you can't afford those bills. Credit cards should only be used for emergencies and two credit cards is the recommended maximum for just about anyone.

Susan is using four credit cards that have varying amounts owed on them. Just paying the minimum monthly payment on each is taking a big chunk out of her budget. However, for now she needs to list the total monthly amount owed. When things are going better, she will concentrate on paying those off.

Loan Payments

Fortunately, Susan has no other loan payments but you might. Do you have a second mortgage or some other loan that is not on a charge card? You will need to budget for these other payments also.

Clothing

This is another item that most people do not budget for and yet you need to have clothes. This is also another item that will vary tremendously from one person to another. Either way, you need to calculate what you think you will need (note that we said need, not want) and put down a monthly amount. This is particularly true if you have children that will be constantly outgrowing clothes and need new clothes, coats, shoes, etc. almost every season. However, just as with your groceries, once you start keeping track of what you are spending on clothes, you will find a lot of ways to save money in this area.

Recreation

Again, most people do not budget for this unless it is for the annual vacation. And some people don't even budget for that but just charge the whole thing on a card.

Although this item is toward the bottom of your list, it is still important and, as with some other items, it will vary tremendously. You could be a person whose idea of recreation is to go for a hike each weekend and, therefore, you do not need to budget much for it. Or you could be a person whose idea of recreation is eating out at least twice a week, going to the movies or renting DVD's, or going to a night club or show each weekend and will, therefore, have to allow a much larger amount in your budget. For now, try to put down a fairly accurate amount. As you see how much you are spending on recreation, you will probably see where you can save quite a bit in this area.

Charity

How many of you actually contribute money to a charity? Or participate in a money-raiser for some charity? Or make a donation at your church each week?

We feel very strongly that you need to create a monthly charity budget to make you feel better and to help the world in general. "Give and ye shall receive." Depending on how you give, your monthly budgeted amount could be any size. Do you go to church every Sunday (or more) and make a donation to the church and other groups each week? This is up to you. But it is important to help others at least a little which will depend on your income.

Pick out a group that you really care about (for instance, we support St. Jude's Hospitals for Children). Can you send a monthly or at least an annual contribution to them (and it is tax deductible). Even $10 once a year will help them. But if you feel you cannot afford even that $10, contact your group of interest and find out other ways you can help. Today most charitable groups have money-raising activities such as walk-a-thons or running events or they put on shows you could attend. There are lots of ways to help without it costing a lot of money. You can even create your own event. Perhaps you and a group of friends go hiking once a month. How about asking each person to give you $2 at each hike that you will contribute to your cause and let these friends know that they will be helping others in an inexpensive and easy way. Tell them about the charity you support so that they can also have that great feeling of helping others.

Everyone complains about their taxes but you might find it interesting to stop and think where your tax dollars are actually going. A lot of non-profit groups such as the arts, museums, symphonies, etc. get huge support from the government (your taxes). Yet if everyone contributed to some group every year, they would not have to depend so heavily on your taxes. You and I know that this would not ever reduce our taxes (Congress would not allow that), but if you want something interesting to suggest to your Congresspeople, suggest doing away with those taxes and making everything dependent on public support. This way you would not be paying to keep the local symphony going that then charges you exorbitant amounts to attend. Only those places that the people want to support will survive.

Savings/Investments

Again, another budget item most people do not stop to think about much less budget for is savings and investments. But investing is your whole future. Not just today but how will you take care of your family and yourself in the future.

We have listed this last because that is where most of you would think of this. "How much have I got left over after playing bills; that is what I will invest this month." And then what happens? You spent everything and do not have anything left over. You need to budget for this also.

What would be ideal is to invest 10% of what you make each month. So, if you only make $4,000 a month you would be investing $400 each month. Obviously, most people cannot afford to do this. But what can you afford? If you invest at least 5% each year, you will be barely keeping ahead of the rate of annual inflation. If you invest 5% each month, you will be matching the percentage of growth that most people get on their investments (pension plans, 401K's, IRA's, Roth IRA's, mutual funds, etc.). Certainly, this is better than doing nothing. For now, put at least a small amount in this spot on your budget. Susan has listed $10 a month. You can work on increasing this amount later so that you will not have financial worries.

Now you need to total up your monthly budget. Next you need to write down what you bring home each month (after taxes). The ideal situation would be to have money left over! Any leftovers will go into the Savings/Investment budget for the month.

But let's be honest here. Most people do not even make a budget and just keep spending till it is all gone and then turn to the charge cards for any additional spending. That is what gets you into debt and could cause you to lose your home, have your car repossessed, ruin your credit rating, and constantly feel deprived.

Therefore, we need to work on this budget to make it add up to what we actually make. There are two ways to do this. One is to not spend as much and the other is to make more money. The easiest is to cut your spending so let's do that one first.

Cutting Costs

The only thing difficult about cutting spending is trying to keep up with the Jones' at the same time. If you are serious about getting out of debt (and you should be), then you have to be serious about cutting back. However, this does not mean you need to deprive yourself for the next ten years. In fact, most people can get out of $20,000 to $30,000 worth of debt in just a year if they really try. And let's face it, it is much easier to cut back on your spending for just one year then it is to look forward to years of deprivation and becoming utterly discouraged.

Obviously you can do little things like turning off the lights when you leave a room and unplugging the TV and computer (this equipment actually continues to use 75% of its usual electricity when just turned off so you need to unplug them) or planning so you can cut back on trips to the store or even carpooling. These certainly will add up but there are other things you can change or cut to create really big monthly savings.

Your mortgage

Now is the time to discuss with yourself and your family which is more important to you, to live in a house or an apartment. You want to keep in mind that your home mortgage is quite often the only and the largest tax deduction you are allowed so you might want to keep it but still cut back on the cost.

First you need to figure out how much your house is costing you. That means adding up what the monthly mortgage is, any additional sewer, county, garbage, water, etc. taxes you pay (usually monthly) plus what you spend on maintenance. Do you pay for the lawn mowing and snow plowing? What about re-painting and re-roofing allowances? What about having emergency electrician and plumbing bills once in awhile? You also need to decide what is important to you. If you really hate all the upkeep of a house, an apartment might be better for you. These are all things you should think about when deciding whether to buy a house or not. If you already own a house, add these things up to get a total of what your house is costing and then check out the monthly cost of an apartment.

If you decide that you want the house, how can you save on that cost? First, you need to read your contract or look at your monthly statement to find out what your interest rate is on the loan. Then plan on spending 2 or 3 hours calling around to see what rate you could get by refinancing that loan. Make sure you ask for and get the dollar amounts in closing costs and fees on that new loan (do not just get the points but the actual dollar amounts). For instance, if you can drop your rate by 2%, this will save you about $200 a month on your mortgage payment. If you already have a mortgage, check with your mortgage lender about refinancing at a lower rate. You will often find that the refinancing fees are drastically reduced or none existent as the lender already has the appraisal, your credit history, etc. on file.

Even if this method will not work for you, there are other ways to use your home mortgage to make more money which we will discuss shortly.

Apartment rental

If you decide to move to an apartment or you already live in one, you need to look at other cost saving options.

Could you get by in a smaller apartment for a couple of years while getting out of debt? Could you double up the kids and go to a two bedroom apartment? Changing from a three to a two bedroom place could save you $200 or more each month.

Could you move to a lower cost area? No, we do not mean a more dangerous run-down neighborhood. However, moving to a smaller town away from the city can reduce your monthly rental as much as $200. Including the additional commute to work, will this create any savings? Rather than assuming that you would end up not saving anything, do the calculations! Adding up the numbers is the only way to see if you would save on this.

An option we are not too fond of is moving back in with your parents. If you come from a very close family (and your spouse does also), then this might be a temporary (one year) option for you until you can get rid of that debt.

Car payments

Whether you own one, two or three vehicles (or more), this item can save you a lot each month. First, if you have two or more cars, do you need that many? Yes, we know it is more convenient, but is it really necessary. Do you and your spouse work close by so you can share a ride to and from work? Cutting back to just one car could save $500 a month or more just in that car payment, registration, insurance, gas and oil, maintenance, etc.

If this is impossible, what about car pooling? Put an ad in your local newspaper for someone to share rides with in your area. Or advertise your own car pool such as, "Looking for people in the Oaks area to carpool to downtown area." Check at work as to who might be living in your area. They can each pay you each week or set up alternating cars so you all share the cost.

If you are driving that long dreamed of sports car, are you ready to look at things in a more mature attitude? Get rid of that car and buy a nice family sedan that will lower your monthly loan payment and cost a lot less to register and insure. And don't forget that most sports cars require specially sized tires that cost up to twice as much as a normal tire.

Do you need a new car? If you buy a good family sedan, keep up with the oil changes and tune ups and, therefore, are able to run that car for 200,000 miles or more, you can save a lot. Let's say you do a lot of driving and put on 20,000 miles a year. That means you could run that car for 10 years but you only have a five year loan on it. So you are making those payments for five years but the next five years free. Every car expert out there will tell you this is the best thing to do particularly if you have a car that you really enjoy.

Can you take public transportation? Keep in mind that, whether you use it or not, your tax dollars built it so why not use it. Figure out what the cost would be and compare that to what you are paying for that extra car.

Groceries

Although the ways to cut your grocery bill will not create as big savings as we have been looking at, they are significant.

First of all, remember that eating out is not groceries and it costs a lot more than cooking does. Do we even need to mention that you can have much healthier meals at home then in most restaurants, let alone fast food places? So make a decision to not eat out for one whole year and get healthier and save money.

However, eating at home can be expensive depending on how you do it. If you depend on frozen or prepared meals, you are wasting a lot of money. Write down what you eat during a typical month. If there are a lot of prepared or frozen meals, either cut those meals out or learn how to make them yourself from scratch. If you do not like to cook, maybe your husband does or one of the kids would like to.

We realize that a lot of men and some women are meat and potatoes types. That meat is a lot more expensive then chicken and causes more health problems than chicken does. Eating fish is very important to your health but can be expensive. Look around your city for an Asian seafood market. Because they cater to the Asian community, their prices are much better. We shop at one where things like tuna and salmon are two-thirds cheaper than the cheapest area grocery store. Find the local bakery and buy day-old bread. Buy paper products and canned goods in bulk. Cut back on desserts. Watch out for farmer's markets as some will charge much higher prices than the supermarket because they are "home grown" or organic.

If you don't like cooking or have never really learned, find five recipes that you and your family really like and learn just those five. Keep in mind that home cooking does not take a lot of time especially if you want to keep it healthy. How long does it take to throw a piece of fish in the oven for 15 minutes, make a salad from lettuce you cleaned over the weekend, and steam a fresh vegetable for 15 minutes (while the fish is cooking)?

We cannot leave this area without talking about gardening. Yes, we personally love gardening as it is impossible to think about problems when you are weeding or, better yet, picking fresh fruits and vegetables. Just for fun, add up how much you spend on lettuce, tomatoes, green peppers and such and then see how much the seeds for those things cost. Even a very small lawn can grow a semi-dwarf apple, orange, pear, or peach tree and still provide shade and beauty. I love going to the grocery store and seeing green peppers (in California) for 69 cents each (or more) when I have a yellow and a red pepper plant at home with tons of peppers that I paid about 50 cents for the seeds.

Phone bill

Probably most of you realize that you can get cell phone service for much less then your line phone costs you. But how many phones do you need? If your teenager just has to have their own phone otherwise everyone will pick on them, then make them pay for it themselves with a part-time job. Yes, they can have a phone but they have to spend 3 hours a week doing gardening work or they have to prepare one family meal each week. Kids who work for things appreciate them much more than the lazy ones who think they will get anything they want in life for free.

TV cable

We realize that some of you choose to not watch TV or do so on a limited basis. However, if you and your family do watch a lot of TV, look at your monthly cable bill! It is not uncommon to be paying $100 or more just for basic cable and a few other stations. And if you get a bigger package, how many of those extra stations do you actually watch? Personally, we watch TV but not a lot as we only have about 5 shows a week that we actually want to see and occasionally a good movie is on (very occasionally).

Trying listing what weekly shows you really want to see (as opposed to the ones you watch because there is nothing else to do). Just cutting back to plain simple basic cable will save you a lot each month. What about turning cable off for one year and saving $1200 or more?

And how many TV sets do you have in your home? How many do you need? And how many of these are attached to cable? If you have young children, they do not need cable to watch enough cartoons each week. If you have teenagers, they should be out doing more physical activity anyway such as mowing the lawn to earn their allowance. If there is a program you particularly want them to watch, they can use the family set.

A certain gentleman I know really wanted a new big screen TV. His wife pointed out to him that they only watched TV a few hours each week. He made a deal with her. They would cancel cable entirely for one year, save that $100 each month and, at the end of a year, they would have enough to buy the new big screen TV. That worked out fine for them.

Keep in mind that keeping up with the Jones' is totally passé. Watching TV is really just a bad habit you have picked up. Try breaking it by going to the library for a good mystery to read (and it's free) or spending more time going for a walk after dinner (it's better for you) or spending a free day as a family at the beach or up in the mountains or fishing (costs a little). How much does getting out of debt mean to you? Are you willing to go that extra distance? Are you willing to enjoy life more?

Insurances, Life, Medical, Car & House

Think of how much money you spend each month betting with your insurance company. They are betting that you are going to be safe and healthy yet you pay them every month because you think you are going to die or be sick or have something terrible happen.

Keep in mind that the financial industry which

includes banks, charge card companies, *and* insurance companies have made bigger profits than any other industry in the last two years (even more than the oil companies have made). Of course, because the insurance industry has so much money, they have a huge lobby in Washington, and they have managed to make some insurances mandatory (and they would like to see all insurances become mandatory).

Because of the laws they have managed to get through Congress, you have to have car insurance. We fully realize that about half of our population (depending on where you live) is driving around without insurance (or a driver's license for that matter), but we do not believe in breaking the law. However, this is an area of huge potential savings. One day we decided to spend three hours checking out different car insurance companies. We ended up with a much better company (they have taken care of problems immediately) and saved close to $4,000 a year (that's for three vehicles). Since then we have cut that even more as we are now down to two vehicles (once the kids are out of school, they are on their own).

Medical insurance is nice if your company is paying for it but more and more businesses need to cut costs and are using health insurance as one way to cut back. If you have children, you need health insurance but if they are now adults and it is only the two of you, is it necessary? Yes and no. Let's say you are paying $200 a month for your health insurance but you decide to instead put that monthly amount into nice safe investments. After all, that is exactly what the insurance company is doing with your money. They put your premiums into investments and become rich off of that money. You can do the same thing (we will talk about saving and investing shortly).

Please remember that most doctor and hospital bills are negotiable if you are paying cash rather than on an insurance plan. A good example is the author of this book. I needed cataract surgery last year that was going to cost close to $8,000. We do not carry any health insurance but instead we have been investing that money. So we sold some stock to raise the amount. However, we found out something very interesting. Because we were paying cash, the doctor and the hospital gave us large cash discounts bringing the whole thing to just $5,000. Also, we are very healthy people (thank you, God). We had not had any major health cost like this in the previous ten years. So we could have been paying for health insurance for ten years at $200 a month for a total of $24,000 and used just $7,000 of it. Instead we invested that $200 a month and ended up using only $5,000 of it in ten years with the rest going toward retirement or any long-term care we might need in the future.

However, as you get older and, therefore, have more illnesses or if you have a history of illness, you may want to shop around for health insurance. Bear in mind that the older you are, the higher your premiums will be.

You definitely need to have house insurance especially if you have a mortgage on your home. There is not much you can do about this, other than increase the deductible, but keep in mind that in recent years many Americans have had a problem with their insurance not covering things like flooding and hurricanes. Of course, even if you carry extra insurance for these acts of God, you are still paying for all the people who do not have the insurance as the government ends up helping them and you pay the bill. If you have been in your house long enough, you may be able to stop the escrow on the insurance. Then you could take this money and invest it yourself to cover any fire, flood, theft, etc. in the future. And if you decide to carry any extra insurance, such as flood insurance, be sure to shop around because premiums can vary widely on these.

Life insurance is necessary if you have children that would need to be taken care of in case of your death. And I mean little children, not your 30 year old son who should be taking care of himself. For this situation you need Term Life Insurance (lasts to a certain age and costs a lot less than whole life insurance). However, once those children are grown, do you need any life insurance? If both you and your spouse work, if anything happens to one of you the other will still have their job and, in some circumstances, could get some social security benefits. If your spouse does not work, then you will want some life insurance to help them if something happens to you. This is Whole Life Insurance (lasts until you die) and is much more expensive.

Your other choice is to invest for the future. Again, by putting the same amount into safe, secure investments, your survivors will always have that money. Keep in mind that putting just $50 a month into your investments instead of into that insurance policy could be worth $100,000 in ten years time. And that is exactly what the life insurance company is doing with your money anyway. The only difference is that, so long as you stay healthy, do not burn down your house, and do not die, they will keep making a huge profit off of you.

Other ways to save

If your house needs painting, can you and the family do it yourselves? How much do you really need to spend on holiday gifts? Stop using the ATM if you are paying a fee for each use. ATM's and charge cards make it much too easy to spend money that, if you took the time to think about it, you would not spend.

The important thing to remember is that you will only be cutting way back until you are out of debt. Just doing the things we have already mentioned could save you $12,000 or much more which would go a long way toward paying off those credit cards.

But just saving money may not be enough. Maybe you need to make more money.

Making More Money

Of course, everyone wants to make more money but along with what money you want you also need to consider what you want your life to be like. We will assume that you also want time and money to do fun things in life. That is why most people have a job, a family and home, and leisure time. But sometimes circumstances mean less time for family and home and leisure and more work time.

That means the first thing most people think of when needing more money (besides asking for a raise that you know you will not get) is to find another part-time job. Just what you need, right? Working even more hours and, instead of being tired every day, now you will be exhausted. However, keep in mind there are two types of part-time jobs. One is working in a store evenings and weekends and the other is starting your own business during that same time. Which one to do will depend on you.

The majority of our population prefers to work for someone else leaving the headaches of the business to the owner while you just do your job and get your paycheck. The other person is one who thrives on challenges and creating something from scratch with your own mind and hands and wants the flexibility of working at their own pace without a boss always ready to criticize.

If you are the entrepreneur type and want to spend your time doing something you really enjoy, you will do what Susan did and think about what you would really like to be doing and start a part-time business doing it.

Starting a business today is very easy as most are home-based. That means you don't have to immediately go into debt by renting office space. Also, by starting out small, you do not have to go into debt by hiring employees. Finally, by doing the advertising yourself, you do not have to have a lot of money to start with.

Susan found a new job but, in order to increase her income, also started her own home-based business by teaching classes in cake decorating as well as making cakes for special occasions. She knew that some of the people who took her classes would decide that the decorating was too difficult and time consuming and would, therefore, end up hiring her to do the job. However, Susan had to set up those classes four to five months ahead which meant she would not be creating income from that for quite a few months. But she could start her own specialty cake business right away. The main problem was how to get the word out.

Fortunately, Margie had a lot of experience in this.

Together Margie and Susan set up a plan (yes, writing another list!) of what needed to be done.

First, Susan was going to write some articles that she could send to newspapers in her area. For instance, one was "Save Money On Your Wedding". Another was "Just 3 Steps to the Cake of Your Dreams". Then she had a basic article on "Decorating a Cake For Any Occasion". Once she got going on this she realized there were lots of articles she could do on this subject. So where does the advertising come in? She created a website for her new business. Then in the last paragraph of each story, Susan would mention, "For free help call 555-555-5555 or go to www.tttt.com". She sent these to all the newspapers and magazines she could find. She also created a quick booklet on her computer with the steps to decorating a cake using three different examples that demonstrated all of the necessary steps. When people called or went online they found out about Susan's upcoming classes and about an inexpensive booklet that would teach them how to do the decorating themselves.

However, Susan didn't stop there. After all, she needed some immediate money. So she also created and sent a press release to all TV and radio stations within 100 miles of her home in order to get on shows for a quick spot demonstrating how to make sugar roses or garlands (TV loves demonstrations) and explaining these things for radio shows. She actually got onto one station for a four minute demo that the station liked so much they asked her to come back the following week for another demo. Of course, each spot showed her phone number and website.

Too many people think that advertising has to cost a lot of money when it really does not. Susan just put in the press release that the demonstration cake would be given to the station personnel. Believe it or not, these local TV and radio stations do not pay very well so any added benefit such as getting free eats is enjoyed.

Charlie and his family also needed to get the word out about their new home business, the Farm Museum. They came up with lots of ways to get on local TV and radio shows. His mother and wife, Diane and Denise, could get onto shows demonstrating home canning in order to "revive this dying American art form" and talked about the daily demonstrations at the museum. Denise and little Joan went on with her pet goat and a chicken talking about what good pets they made - - and talked about visiting the museum.

With the help of two well-placed signs in town and just two of these media spots, Charlie and his family hosted 65 paying guests that first weekend their museum was open for business. They quickly expanded by contacting schools about special rates and special hand-on demonstrations for school classes. Eventually they could expand to offer a one-hour presentation for all family members through these same schools.

Helen did not have a financial problem as she had a good teaching position. Therefore, she actually paid for small advertisements in the paper about the travel group she had set up through her church, the hiking group for singles, the exercise group to "lose weight together", and the reading group at the library. This meant that she could start those group within the week. She also found that a lot of people attended one group, found out about the others, and joined them also. And this meant she was meeting lots of new people who could introduce her to single men who liked the same things she did and she was making new friends she enjoyed being with. If you have friends to do things with, life will not be so lonely while looking for that one right person.

Keep in mind that virtually anything you like to do you can find a part-time job in or even create your own business. Do you like to fly kites? You can teach classes on building and flying kites. Do you love gardening? Offer classes on growing healthy food, cooking with fresh herbs, flower arranging, etc. Do you love woodworking? How about repairing other people's old furniture or teaching them how to do it themselves?

However, finding or creating another job is not the only way to bring in more money.

Susan decided to put the two kids into one bedroom and rent out the third room to a local college student for $500 a month. The kids weren't wild about sharing a room but Susan made sure they understood it was only going to be for one year. She also found that, after 10 years of marriage, she had a lot of things she never used (including her ex-husband's things he did not take with him) and had a huge yard sale that netted over $700 in one weekend.

If Helen wanted to make some extra money, rather

than offering the groups for free, she could charge a small amount to belong to the group to cover her own expenses.

Joan, being a very smart 11 year old, quickly figured out that she could sell feed to the kids at her petting zoo to cover the cost of the feed but also make some extra money for herself. And her grandmother, Diane, found that people not only wanted to see her making a pie from scratch but also wanted to buy them to take home.

And if you really cannot think of what to do with the thing you love doing, email us at ELPBooks@aol.com (mention in the subject line "book") and we can help you with brainstorming great ideas.

Creating Your Short Term Dream Life

We have been talking about major problems that need to be solved fairly quickly (within the next one to twelve months). But most people have other smaller problems that also need to be fixed and soon. Life is not just about work and earning a living.

Helen needed to meet new people and take time to enjoy life. She did it by joining groups and creating her own groups. This is always a good thing to do.

But what if you already have a family and you and your spouse both work full-time? Then you have the house to take care of and the kids to raise, and what time do you have leftover for yourself? Or maybe you find that between the two jobs and the housework and the kids activities and school, there is no real family time.

Family time and *self* time are very important in life. And, again, this does not happen by itself. After all, it is a lot easier to come home from a hard day at work, eat a delivered pizza and then flop in front of the TV. Believe it or not, it takes some energy and planning if you want to have fun. You need to plan for it. The best way to start is to think small.

Plan at least 10 hours each week that will be family time (not including meals). If one of the kids has a game on Saturday morning, make it a family affair. Everyone goes to support that child. Remind the whiner that the other family members will be there to support his next recital or game (this includes reminding your spouse of all the support they will be getting also). If church is important in your family, make sure everyone attends every Sunday morning together.

You have all heard of the "honey-do" list and that is also an important list. These are short-term things that need to be done this week or this month. Again, the purpose of this list is to write everything down so you know what needs to be done *and* so you can feel good every time you cross something off. This list can include everything from "pay the bills" this week to things you want to do such as "tear up the old carpet and lay down hardwood flooring".

Keep in mind that the other members of your family need some input into all of this planning also. Have a family meeting once a month to get ideas of what the others would like to do (this could be short or long term planning). If one wants to go swimming, how about planning a few hours for the whole family to go to the beach together. Maybe your daughter really wants to redo her bedroom; this is a project the whole family can help with from the painting to hanging curtains.

Note that we did not include meal time as part of these family efforts. The whole family should have at least five meals a week together. This means if Dad has to work late on Tuesday, then we will make sure we have dinner together on Saturday. Also, meal time does not mean just sitting down to eat together. You know there is always preparation to a meal. Plan from 1 to 1½ hours for meal times. Half of that will be where everyone gets together to create the meal and the other half is eating *and talking* time. Yes, there is still clean up time but that should be shared in a family with everyone taking turns cleaning up. Everyone has their own list of chores. And we do mean LIST. The biggest problem in getting anyone to do what they have agreed to do is that they easily forget (or pretend to forget). They cannot forget when there is an actual list posted for everyone to see all the time.

You and each member of your family also need a little alone time to do whatever you want. Everyone knows this but it is another thing to actually do it. The kids do this by hanging out in their room with the door closed and the music blaring. But you need this alone time, too. This is another place where you need a list of what you want to do for yourself.

Susan made a list including cooking, painting, playing the piano, and traveling. Charlie and his family were keeping the farm together and still doing the things they liked such as Denise being with the kids more, Diane getting to cook more, and Joan having more pets for her petting zoo. Helen had too much alone time so she took all the things she liked doing and created groups so she had companionship doing those things.

You should do something you love doing every single day for at least five minutes. Five minutes is not a long time. Anyone can spare five minutes in a day. So what do you love to do?

Play an instrument? Call a friend? Read a book in peace and quiet? Sit in the sun and get some vitamin C for five minutes? This five minutes can change your whole outlook on life. It is a form of mediation wherein you forget about everything else and take the time to breath deeply and relax. Fun is important because it brings a smile to your face which actually releases chemicals in your body that make you feel better. If you truly cannot think of anything else to do, meditate for five minutes a day. Just sit comfortably, close your eyes, and picture you laying in a hammock under a big shade tree with a small stream gurgling nearby. And breath deeply! If you fall asleep, no big deal, it just means you needed a nap anyway.

And having fun does not have to cost a lot. In fact, most of the time it is virtually free. Having a picnic at the nearest park does not cost anything extra. Going for a walk through your neighborhood or park is free. Collecting seashells or leaves or interesting rocks is free. How much does it cost to listen to music or read a book? And some things cost a small amount such as visiting a museum, taking a dance class, or going camping.

Maybe your alone time means doing something special for yourself. How much more special can you get then taking care of yourself. We are not just talking about having a facial or spa treatment, but how about exercising (it will do wonders for your face). However, this will take more than 5 minutes a day. What do you like to do the most or dislike the least? If you love to jog, then work up to 2 miles a day. If your knees cannot take the jogging, then walk. 10,000 steps a day means you can eat the same amount and still lose weight. If you think about it carefully, do you really want to end up with diabetes or a heart problem? You know you would rather live healthy.

Financial planning means that, by using a little of your time, you can pay off your debts much quicker then by sending in that minimum payment each month, live comfortably on less and you can have time and money to do the fun things in life. And once those debts are paid off, you will have all that extra money for your *big* dreams.

We have been talking about what to do if you do not have enough income. But supposing you have the income for your day-to-day living but you have big dreams that are going to cost a lot? Or you have now paid off your debts and end up with extra money each month? How are you going to ever get to spend two weeks in Italy?

Chapter 5
Long Term Life Planning

Everyone should have dreams otherwise where is your life going. Once you have the day-to-day plans set and you are working on getting that new job or starting that new hobby, it's time to start thinking about the future. This is the big life plan. Who should be doing this? Everyone! From the time you start high school and onward you should be planning your future.

Obviously what you want and need will continue to change over your life but that is all the more reason to have a plan so you *can* change it whenever you need to.

This list could consist of getting a degree, going to Europe (or seeing your own country first), creating a retirement fund, writing and publishing a book, planning your wedding, building a home, etc. These are things that usually will be done in the future because you can't afford them right now or now is just not the right time for these things. News flash! If you don't plan for these things, they will never happen!

**"The future belongs to those who will
prepare for it."
Optimist Club**

Encourage your children and any other family members to create their own lists also. And, of course, teach them how to plan to accomplish these things.

So here is another list, what you want to accomplish

in your life, you need to write down and hang up where you can see it every day. But how are you going to get these things? This takes planning also.

Some of these things will take a great deal of money (such as going to Europe) and you will have to create a long-term financial plan for these. But you would be surprised at how many things can be done quite inexpensively.

For instance, if you want to travel, it is just a matter of planning the trip. Wherever it is you want to go, you will need to plan when you want to go. Set a date to aim for whether it is next year or ten years from now. This does not necessarily mean you will be ready by that date, but at least it gives you something to plan for. Otherwise, you will keep saying to yourself, "some day" and then some day never seems to arrive.

Next you need to put down how long the trip will be: a long weekend, a week, two weeks, a month? From this information you can calculate how much it is going to cost. Today it is very easy to go online and find out how much a hotel will cost, your airline ticket, car rental or train fare, etc. But keep in mind that what you usually find online are the more expensive places that can afford to advertise. You might need to do some of your own investigating, especially if you are on a tight budget, by contacting the Bureau of Tourism to get a more complete listing or going online and checking out hostels and guest houses.

You need to decide what type of person you are.

Are you the one who will only travel if it is first class all the way? Or are you the one that is more interested in seeing things then where you sleep at night? If you are budget minded (and we think everyone should be), than do more research to find out the true cost. For instance, let's say you want to visit England. There are guides in the bookstores that list expensive, medium, and cheap places to stay. Or contact the Bureau of Tourism for lists of inexpensive places. Yes, this all takes time but it also adds to the fun. We can guarantee you that half of the fun is planning on going to Disney World next year. The other half is actually being there.

The same planning needs to go into whatever else you want. Where will you go for that college degree? How much will it cost? Everyone knows that weddings can be just as meaningful on a tiny budget as they can on a huge budget but you still need to know how much it is going to cost you. Do you want to have your own home? How much will you need? Do you have children that may want to go to college? You will need to budget for that. These are things that you could plan and budget for in the coming two years or ten years. Or, as with college, you may have 18 years to budget for it. You can save for these things by setting your budget and then putting so much money into a savings account each month. Or you can get much better growth for your dollars by investing.

Investing for your future must be on everyone's list whether you are 25 years old or 80, whether married or single, whether you have children or not. This is an absolute necessity not only so you can live comfortably when you retire but so you will have emergency funds for that surgery you never planned on or long-term care, or when you are suddenly unemployed and are in danger of losing your home.

After doing your research you will find that some of these long term things that you want you cannot possibly afford. Maybe you could put away $2 a month into a savings account to go to Europe some day, but it would be better to wait until you have your short-term financial planning under control so that you have extra money at the end of each month. Therefore, some of these things will remain on your long-term life planning list.

However, some of these things, such as a child's education if they are getting very near to college age and investing for your future need to be started right away.

Let's look at the emergency situation first. Your son is in high school and there isn't much time to save up for college.

Chapter
Long Term Financial Planning

Education

Charlie's son Mike is a high school freshman and wants to become an architect. However, his first problem is helping his family save the family farm. Well, three months after the first meeting with Margie, it looks like this problem has been solved. The museum and all its other money-makers are doing well and the family is enjoying not only having these visitors but they are also enjoying living with less stress.

Denise quit her job and has already taken three school groups on farm tours including what is involved in getting milk from the cows to the children's dinner table, Diane has taught them how butter used to be made as well as how it is made today, and Dickie is getting to run the day-to-day business even though he is still in school. Mike's advertising efforts have gotten Denise and Diane on the morning and evening news programs which has brought in a lot of weekend guests. However, little Joan gets bragging rights because her petting zoo is the most popular part of the tour. She has even expanded into bringing home new animals from the local Humane Society. Plus, because the news media loves stories that involve kids and animals, Joan has been doing her own appearances on radio and TV and in the newspapers.

All Charlie needed to do was expand a perfectly good business in order to bring in more profit. Of course, this is a small family business and Charlie will never get rich from this, but the family only cares about keeping the farm and making a decent living. This is great for Dickie who will get to inherit the farm and spend the rest of his life doing what he loves. However, Mike has other things on his mind. He really wants to become an architect. But will he be able to afford it?

As Charlie has found out, college is not for everyone. Keep in mind that colleges were originally created in the Colonial days for rich sons to further a general education that would create the illusion that they were better than the common folk. However, starting in the early 1900's, parents saw college as a way for their sons (and eventually daughters) to earn more money. Unfortunately, today a lot of parents and teachers feel that college is absolutely necessary to become a success in life (make more money).

However, statistics do not support this as it depends on whose numbers you use. For instance, the government statistics which includes everyone from local to Federal employees, will track college graduates to find that they get higher paying jobs than non-graduates. However, if you look at the CEO's and owners of the profitable companies, you will find that the majority of them do not have a degree. Why? Because a lot of people are leaders and self-starter entrepreneurs. These people, both men and women equally, are starting businesses and being very successful.

Just look at the number of housewives who are now starting home businesses and than expanding as they become more and more successful.

We are not saying that one should not go to college.

We are saying that college is not for everyone. Rather than push high school students to attend college, why not see if they are really suited for it. We have worked for three state universities and learned that 75% of all incoming college freshman do not graduate from college because of failing or dropping out. The interesting part of this is that the schools know this is going to happen when they accept the students. Why? Because this is how colleges and universities make money. Without enough students, the schools would fail. Keep in mind that the title "non-profit" does not mean that they do not make a profit. It means that if they make more than what their operating costs are, then they use the additional "profit" to increase wages, usually for the higher echelons. This is why they are constantly looking to the tax payer and former graduates to fund the new buildings.

If you have a child that is highly intelligent and capable of doing the advanced work and actually wants to do this, then go for it. But if your child is applying to colleges just to satisfy you or what others expect from them, they could end up with a college degree (or flunking out) and working for someone else for the rest of their lives in a job they do not even like.

Dickie loves the farm and will be very successful with it. He has learned from his family how to pull together and support each others endeavors. He is getting hands-on training and learning that will help him in the future. Just because he is not going to continue school after high school does not mean he will stop learning. He has already learned that to be successful in any business you have to keep innovating and changing.

Mike wants that degree and his parents (and his whole family) want this for him. But how will they pay for it? Through long-term planning and long-term financial planning. And Margie knows how to do this.

They could start a savings account at their credit union for Mike. But that is not going to have enough growth to help his education. They could start a tuition savings plan that will also not help much. But Margie has a better way.

They learned that you do not have to have a lot of money to invest and you do not have to just hand over your money to a broker or your employer to invest however they see fit. Through research at the library, Charlie and Denise found very safe, secure companies that have a very long history of safety and growth (usually 100 years or longer). They knew they wanted to invest only in safe stock because Mike is too close to college and they cannot afford to lose this money. They called these safe growth companies to find out which ones offer a direct cash purchase program that will allow them to invest their money directly through the company without going through a broker. And, very importantly, they found out that they could do this on very little money. For instance, Charlie invested $250 in Costco Wholesale Corporation. They had been shopping there for years and knew (just from trying to find a parking space) that Costco did very well. However, at the library in The Value Line, they found that this company had been averaging a 55% annual growth in the value of their stock. After that first investment, Mike continued to add another $50 each month to his account from his farm earnings (although he knew that he could add as little as $25 each month). With this type of investing, in three years his account could be worth $10,000 or more. This along with taking some student loans, applying for Pell grants and scholarships as well as working part-time while in college should get him through without any loans or very minimal loans.

We have to stress the idea of students working part-time while in college. One of the things we found from the universities we worked at is that students who had to pay at least 50% of their costs themselves were more likely to complete their education as opposed to students whose parents were paying for everything. There is a mistaken belief that students will do better if they can devote all of their time to studies. Reality is they do not spend enough time on studies and, if they do not have to work for it, they really do not care about that degree. If that degree really means a lot to them, they can work part-time and do the school work, too. As with any work, it all depends on how much it means to you.

Mike could spend his time regretting that he had not started doing this investing sooner but looking backward will not move him forward. Besides he has now learned how to invest for the rest of his life.

And what did Charlie and Denise learn? That they could start investments for Joan now and have seven years to save for her veterinarian or animal science degree. They have taught their children that they will get paid (weekly allowances) for their hard work and that they can choose how much of that money to put away for their future. Keep in mind that a student can earn up to $600 without having to pay taxes on it. From that up to $7,825 a year they will be required to pay only 10% tax. However, because these kids work on their family farm, they are not considered employees and do not have to be paid minimum wages. Keep in mind that any family run business can benefit your children without creating more taxes for you.

Education should continue throughout your life. Each individual whether in high school or older must decide for themselves as to whether a college degree is what they really want to do.

The same thing goes for buying a house. Home ownership is not for everyone.

Buying A Home

It has always been the American dream to own your own home. Starting with the first settlers in this country, the idea was to leave poverty behind and move to a new country where anyone could work hard, save their earnings, and buy their own home. This usually meant buying their own farm. But not necessarily. Keep in mind that a lot of the settlers were already trained in other things. For instance, a man in Jamestown was a trained blacksmith (something the other settlers needed) and his dream was to not have to work for a master in the old country but to have his own business.

However, as with every thing in life, things change. Unfortunately, sometimes people do not keep up with the changes. Just as with that college degree, you have to figure out what is right for you.

Do you enjoy living in an apartment? Keep in mind that a lot of people, particularly young singles, enjoy the companionship of having others around them (usually other young singles). A lot of people like not having to do things like mowing the lawn and making sure the driveway is plowed in the winter. They do not want to have to paint the house or pay out over a thousand dollars to have someone paint it for them. They like being able to just call management when the toilet is broken. And a lot of people like paying out less money each month for rent rather than a high mortgage payment. There are advantages to living in an apartment situation.

However, if you enjoy mowing and shoveling and painting and re-roofing and fixing, then you might want to buy a house. Keep in mind that your home is a huge investment in time and money, the largest you will probably ever make in your life. This means you need to be able to get your investment back. If you buy a house and then three years down the road you need to move to a new job, will you be able to sell that house for what you have put into it? Again, times have changed. It used to be that people settled in a town, got a job for life and bought a home. That is not the way life is today. Our population is the most mobile group ever to live in this country. 70% of our population moves more than the settlers on wagon trains did. The current national average for a homeowner to remain in the same house is less than 7 years. You certainly do not want to find yourself in a situation where you cannot sell your house and make at least a small profit on it. And you cannot automatically assume that your property will appreciate or grow in value. Twenty years ago you could buy property and know that in ten years it would be worth a lot more. Times have changed. Depending on what is going on with our economy, both local and federal, that property might be worth less ten years down the road. If you are going to *invest* in a home, then you need to make sure it appreciates or grows in value.

A lot of people think that finding the right place is the first thing to do. Wrong. Making sure you have good reasonable financing is the first thing to do.

It is easy to find a house and then have your real estate agent find you a loan but this may not be in your best interest. That agent does not have to make the monthly payments and does not care if it is a balloon loan or an interest only loan that could ruin you. They will not be around in five years when you have to come up with the remaining balloon payment. They will not be there when you sell the house but have not created any equity in it (interest only loan) and end up having to sell the house and have no profit to buy another one with or, much worse, lose money on the sale and have to pay the remainder of the mortgage out of your pocket.

This means you have to do the work to find the best deal. Investing means having your money work for you, not just sit there doing nothing. Therefore, you should be looking for a loan for at least 90% of the price with a 10% down payment. However, if you have more then 10% saved, it might be in your interest to provide a higher down payment in order to borrow less and have a smaller monthly payment. However, keep in mind that if you do have more saved, you might want to think about investing that for your future which includes any bad times that come along.

Remember that we are talking about your home. This should not be a risky investment that you could end up losing. This should be a good safe investment.

You need to contact credit unions and banks for the better deals keeping in mind that your credit union will usually give you the best deal. To check out the current prevailing rates online go to Bankrate.com. You should be looking for a low interest rate with a small down payment and, usually, a 30 year fixed rate mortgage to keep your payments as low as possible. However, there are other fees you will also need to check for such as application fees, closing costs, title insurance, surveyor costs, bank appraiser cost, inspections, and possible legal fees. Keep in mind that the lender is in this to make money. Therefore, if they offer a lower interest rate, they will make their profit off the other miscellaneous things that people do not think to ask about such as fees and points (a point is 1% of the amount borrowed, 2 points is 2%, etc.).

Aside from credit unions and banks, there are also federal, state and community financing programs that require little or no money down. We are not talking about lending institutions that require no money down. These programs are usually very bad for you as you never build any equity in your house and you keep paying that mortgage payment forever. There is no central clearing house for these government programs but check with your local housing authorities for them. Some of these provide special rates if you are buying a historical building or buying in a redevelopment area where the town wants people to buy run down houses and fix them up to reclaim that area and make it a more desirable place to live.

The lender is interested in your credit rating meaning do you have a good history of paying everything on time, do you have sufficient income to support this loan, and do you have a sufficient down payment. If you do not have these three things, do not buy a house as you will not be able to support the loan in bad times (i.e. you lose your job, have huge medical problems, etc.).

From these three things, your credit rating, income, and down payment amount, your lender will tell you how much they are willing to lend you. Now you have the information you need to find a house in the price range you can afford.

We assume you are reading this book because you want to be financially successful in your life. That means you need to get a bargain which depends on finding someone who needs to sell quickly or buying when real estate values have dropped or buying a house that needs a little fixing up. A lot of people seem very interested in "moving up" by starting small and then selling that first home to buy a bigger and better house. However, if you are interested in doing other things in your life, then keep in mind that one of the richest men in this country, Warren Buffett, still lives in the same house purchased a long time ago. You do not have to keep moving up. Building your wealth means not wasting your money. Some of the richest people live rather frugally and that is one of the reasons that they have accumulated so much wealth. Building your own dream life means putting your money into the things that really mean the most to you in life rather than spending it on unnecessary items.

Do your own research online. It is nice to dream of finding that house that is perfect for you as it is. But you can get a much better deal if photos show an old dark kitchen that you could freshen up with a little yellow paint on the walls or a front yard that needs a little landscaping. Is it in a good location? This sounds like an oxymoron - finding a fixer-upper in a good area! But it happens a lot especially when our economy is not so good.

Or maybe you do find the place that is perfect the way it is and has a low price because the economy is not doing well (or the real estate market is down) and they have to move to a new job and must sell now.

Once you have found the right place, you need to negotiate a good deal. Your first offer should be substantially below the asking price but do not go unreasonably low.

Some of you are thinking, "But prices are so high right now and they are getting those prices. I can't underbid everyone and expect to get what I want!" The answer to this is very simple.

If prices are high, a seller's market, then don't buy a house. Does it make sense to buy anything at top dollar that will not be worth that amount next year? Your home is an investment and it must therefore appreciate in value. If the market prices for homes in your area are too high, then don't buy. Go out and rent for awhile till the prices come down. Meanwhile, you can continue to save more for your down payment. And prices will come down. As with everything in life, real estate is a cycle of ups and downs.

So let's assume it is a normal market, that is, there are the same number of people that want to buy as want to sell and prices have not been artificially inflated. This means you can offer less than the asking price. Now you can negotiate. They will come back with a slightly lower price then they originally asked and you can counter with somewhere in between. But do not go above what you think this house is truly worth or above what your research has shown you to be the current prices in that area. And keep in mind what the house will be worth to you if you know you will be living in it for at least the next 10 years. The longer you stay there, the more chance you have to build equity in it through normal appreciation in the area, through appreciation from having paid off more of the loan, and from appreciation due to home improvements you have made.

Actual worth will be determined through research. Go online to find out what the average house in that particular area is going for by putting in that zip code. If it is a normal real estate market, you do not need to go above that amount. If you are looking for a good deal on a fixer-upper, you don't want to approach the average home price because you will have to put more money in to fix the place up.

Keep in mind that no one should buy real estate quickly. If it is a fast selling market, then don't play the game. You want to buy when those sellers are trying to find someone to buy. This will also give you more time to think logically and make a better decision.

Your home is a huge investment that you will be able to use for a lot of things in the future. As you fix up the place and as time goes by, it will become worth more money (you will build equity in it). This means that if you need to you can sell it and make a good profit from it. However, this equity helps in other ways. Perhaps you have a business but need money to make it grow bigger and better or you now want to buy some rental property to create income for you. You can take a second mortgage on your home to provide that needed cash. Perhaps you retire and, if you are over 62, you run into a lot of medical expenses that you cannot afford. You can take a reverse mortgage on the house, continue to live in it, but the bank will be paying you each month. Yes, your home is a lot more than just a house.

But the last situation, retiring and not having enough to live on, will not happen to you because you are going to plan and invest for your future.

Charlie and Denise love the farm but even at 40 years old they are beginning to have a few more aches and pains than they used to. And Charlie's mother, Diane, is only 60 but needs cataract surgery. She spent her entire life working the farm and has no savings set aside. Charlie needs to plan for his own retirement when he cannot do the necessary work and turns the farm over to Dickie. And he needs to make sure that future emergency's such as medical situations can be taken care of.

Chapter 7
Saving For the Future

Charlie now has the farm on a sound footing wherein all the bills are being paid. He and Mike are saving for Mike's college program. Now he needs to plan his and Denise's retirement.

Susan has found a job to pay the bills but wants to start her own business and she has to plan for her children's education as well as for emergency's. She knows she does not want to be in the same situation again of losing her job and having no way to pay the bills.

Helen has been taking care of her retirement the good old-fashioned way, through her school retirement account. She has been putting money away in her pension plan as well as into an IRA. She realizes this will not make her rich, but as she will have been doing it for 45 years by the time she retires, she should have a decent amount. She also has health insurance at work. But could she be doing more?

How do rich people become rich? They do not spend any more than they absolutely have to and they invest their money in safe large growth stock. Do the Kennedy's put their money into a mutual funds or IRA's? Of course not. They carefully pick and choose safe companies so that their money will not suddenly disappear and growth companies so that the money they invest will keep on growing for them. You can do exactly the same, just at a smaller level of investment. And obviously, the younger you start doing this, the better off you will be. But it is never too late to create a nest egg.

We have already talked about investing directly in safe growth companies for educational purposes as well as for your retirement and other emergencies. And we have talked about investing in a house that can help you financially when you are older. There are lots of ways to save for the future, some better than others, but there is one that a lot of people do not think about. Starting your own business.

Starting and Building Your Own Business

Running a business is not for everyone. Are you good at facing the unknown and uncertainty of owning your own business? Do you like the satisfaction you get from creating something from scratch? Is there something that you really enjoy doing so much that you are willing to take some risk to do it full time? If your answer is a resounding NO, then you need to find a regular job that will give you fulfillment in life while supporting the family. But if you said YES, then you need to create a plan.

Charlie already had a business. He just needed to make it grow in order to prosper. Helen has a job she loves. But Susan would really like to be her own boss. She remembers the times she has made suggestions to her former boss which he ignored only to realize that she had a good idea. Unfortunately, he was not the type of man that could say, "You know, that was a good idea. Do you have any more ideas?" No, as far as he was concerned, Susan was just a secretary who didn't even have a college degree. He knew that she knew nothing about running a business.

Of course, he did not stop to think that she had run a

household for ten years by herself or that she had learned a lot during those ten years of working for other bosses and learning from their mistakes (which were plentiful).

But now Susan had her opportunity. More importantly, she now realized that she needed to depend on herself and not the whims of other people. She had a good full-time job that paid the bills, barely! But she wanted more. Within a few weeks of starting as the business manager at the restaurant, she realized that she had lots of ideas on how to run it more efficiently, more cost effectively, and better. But this time she was not going to even attempt to discuss it with the boss.

By the third week on the new job, Susan found herself starting to plan things in her head. But she found it too difficult to keep track of all of her ideas that way so she sat down one evening and wrote down a plan.

She started with the ideas she had already come up with when talking with Margie. So her list began with 'teach classes' and under that she made a list of all the colleges and universities and school districts in her county. These were places she could contact about offering cooking classes. Then she made a list of where she could advertise her own cake catering service. Of course, she did not have extra money for this but she still listed newspapers, radio stations, TV stations, and her own flyer.

You might notice that Susan is really doing exactly what Charlie and his family did with his on-going business. He started teaching people by having the farm tours and Denise and Joan were doing radio and TV interviews as well as getting in the newspapers. And without paying for it. They knew that to get free news media coverage you have to give people information that they need and can use. Therefore, when the economy went into a recession and not as many people could afford to go to their museum, Denise did news releases and interviews on how to start your own garden to save on the high cost of tomatoes and did demonstrations of how to freeze your produce to save on groceries. Of course, they would mention their live demonstrations and free printed information available at the Farm Museum. When the economy is good and people do have spending money, they stressed the fun of hay rides, the petting zoo, teaching kids where their pizzas come from and getting more people to visit Joan's pizza garden (a round garden where each slice is filled with part of a pizza, as in tomatoes, basil, wheat, green peppers, etc.)

Susan created a good proposal letter for the schools. She then called each school to find out if they offered non-credit courses and, if so, who should she contact to submit a proposal for a new class. However, she quickly ran into a problem. To demonstrate cooking she needed a kitchen and the schools did not have that type of facility, only regular class rooms. So Susan changed the proposal to offering the classes in her own home with the school advertising it in their catalog, taking the registrations and keeping a percentage of the attendance fees. The classes would not pay her a lot but she knew that quite a few people would decide to hire her to make that special cake rather than try it themselves.

Susan also created a flyer about her business with some pictures of her best cakes and price ranges. She always had these with her and handed them out in her classes. She also found that TV news programs (on slow news days) loved having her do a quick spot demonstrating how to make sugar roses or how to create a heart shaped cake for Valentine's Day without buying a special pan.

Susan started her classes simply teaching people how to do these things but quickly learned that her students wanted everything written out for them. So Susan started writing her first cook book on decorating cakes for special occasions.

She also hired a high school student (she was on a tight budget but could hire a student for very little) to create a website for her business that not only advertised her classes and her cakes but also had information on ordering Susan's monthly newsletter that would feature a different cake and how to create it in each issue.

So why are Charlie's farm and Susan's home business an investment, other then the fact that they are investing their money into it? Because they now have income that they can control and make it grow as much or as little as they want. They can work hard doing something they love and know that they will profit from it. This means not having to worry about working at something you hate, being fired or laid off, or even retirement as they can keep on doing these things (and expanding their businesses) for as long as they want to, even after they reach retirement age. Susan can do all the cooking she wants to even when she is 80 years old - and probably get some great publicity from being so active at 80!

However, even Charlie and Susan need to save for their future and, even if you work for someone else and have a retirement plan, you still need to do your own saving and investing. And Susan wants to tour Europe some day.

Investing

Helen is doing the right thing by investing in her employer's retirement plan and in an IRA (Individual Retirement Account). Doing even this type of investing that actually creates small returns is better than doing nothing for your future. But what else could she do? And Charlie and Susan definitely need to protect their future. Even Mike at 15 and Joan at 11 need to be saving for their future college education.

There are quite a few choices for you. You could put your money into a savings account at the bank but, at today's very low interest rates, you won't see much growth. You can get safety but with small growth through a Certificate of Deposit. In fact, you should always have some money in these two types of savings for when you need money very quickly. You should have enough in one or both of these types of investments to cover 3 months of your living expenses in case of job loss or medical problems. This should be part of your short-term financial planning.

The rest of your life falls under long-term financial planning and, again, you have several choices. Investing in any mutual fund situation through your work such as a pension plan or 401K plan is better than doing nothing. However, these plans often lose your money during bad times, have relatively low earnings (averaging 5%) during good times, and you could possibly lose everything if your employer closes or discontinues the plan. But, as we said before, doing something is better than doing nothing.

Just as we recommend you taking charge of your own life by planning your life, you should take care of your own money. Would you tell your child to go out into the streets and find a complete stranger and give all of their money to this stranger to take care of for them? Yet that is what most Americans do every day. They talk to a stranger (a broker they have never known before) and then give their money to them. Your logic tells you that this person just wants to make money off of your money (and as much as possible) but you find yourself thinking, "I don't know what to do. I don't have the time for this. I need to pay someone to do this for me."

We have already talked about investing in yourself by starting your own business. You can also invest in real estate for rental purposes to provide additional income even when you retire. But every person should do is what the Rockefeller's and Kennedy's do - invest directly into companies that have a long history of safety and growth. Think about it. Very rich people do not put there money into a mutual fund situation. They find the very safest best companies they can to put their money into. Warren Buffett finds a company he likes and then buys it, figuratively and literally! Well, you and I cannot do that. But we can invest in those companies.

For instance, you could buy $500 worth of stock directly through Target Corporation and have a 50% annual growth in value (averaged over past 10 years). Then continue to put in $50 a month and see your account grow by almost 100% a year due to the normal growth of a good stock plus your continuing deposits into your account. But what if you cannot afford that initial $500? This is a company that will actually waive the initial $500 if you sign up for a plan guaranteeing that you will make periodic purchases of stock of $50 or more. And there are other good safe companies that you can buy as little as one share to start with and put in as little as $10 each month.

How much are you putting into your pension plan right now and only averaging 5% growth? Our type of investing costs you less (no broker fees or extremely minimal fees), you have complete control as to buying and selling whenever you want, and you can always sell stock and receive the cash within 5 days of the sale.

How much will you need for retirement? Besides your weekly and monthly budget, you will also need a long-term financial plan. This will cover things you want to get or do in the future such as buying a house some day, sending your kids to college, having money available for medical and other emergencies, as well as your retirement income. Some of these things are finite such as planning for college. You can find out how much this is going to cost and figure out how much you need to put away each month and for how many years to get that amount. Planning what you will need for retirement is more fluid but you still need a plan.

It is very much like your monthly budget but you will need to do calculations for future costs that you do not know how much they will be yet. Again, list all the expected costs such as mortgage payment or rental, car expenses, groceries, utilities, etc. Then figure out how much you are worth. This includes checking with Social

Security to see what your expected payment will be when you retire, check any pension or savings plans to see what they should be worth at retirement, and calculate what your personal investments will be worth.

If your retirement income will not be enough to cover your expenses, how can you increase what you are putting away to cover all of those costs? This includes putting more into those savings plans, what income will you have from your own business that you can continue to operate after you retire, or income from any rental property.

But this financial plan will vary a lot more than your monthly budget will. Monthly expenses are pretty well set and you know what to expect each month. Retirement budgets can change a lot between now and age 65 (or 70). This is normal. All it means is that you should plan on spending one evening once a year to go over your retirement plan(s) and expenses to see where you stand and if any adjustments need to be made. Just as what you want to attain in life will change over the years, what you want and need for retirement will also change with time.

Today you might be single and dreaming of traveling throughout the world but tomorrow you could find your soul mate and find yourself thinking about college education for the kids and just trying to see the USA instead of the whole world. That is why writing all of these plans down works so well. It is very easy to cross something off and write in something else whenever you need to.

There is one more long-term plan you need to make

that we did not mention on the front cover. After all, we certainly do not want to discourage people from reading this book. The other unmentionable thing you need to plan is your death. Hey, it happens to everyone!

Most people choose to ignore this situation figuring that when they die their unpaid bills, house, investments and whatever else is left will be someone else's problem to worry about. However, assuming that you have worked hard to attain some measure of comfort in life, you might want to help people out after you are gone.

This means creating a will. This does not have to be difficult as you can go into any office supply store and they have kits with all the forms you need. But there are some other things you might care about. Make sure that a person or loved one knows where your will is kept and along with it include information such as who to notify of your death. I know I would be devastated if my very good friend passed away and no one told me about it. You will also need to include a list of any insurance policies, investments or pension plans, home ownership papers as well as vehicle ownership papers. List your CPA and lawyer if you have these. Also, if you truly want that "certain item" to go to a specific person, consider giving it to that person now to assure that heirloom ring actually goes to your eldest son.

And, if it is important to you, what do you want done when you pass. What type of funeral do you want, do you already have a plot and where is it, what type of funeral service do you want? Again, you may not care about any of this but it would make things easier for someone else.

Chapter 8
Planning Your Life

It has just taken a lot of pages to explain everything that you need to do in order to build your dream life but it does not take very long to actually do it. All of this planning should not take more then two evenings to do. You should plan on a once a year update (we find that New Year's Day is easy to remember and gets the New Year off on a good footing). What do you need to do?

Create a list of things you would like to get or do during the coming year.

Create a monthly budget including saving for these above things.

Create a list of what you want in your future from a home to hobbies.

Create a budget to attain these long-term needs and wants.

List what you will need when you retire.

Create a monthly and annual investing plan to get there.

That's just 6 steps to building your dream life.

Susan now has a good job managing a restaurant that has taught her even more about running her own business effectively. She has a calendar that keeps track of all of her order due dates for cakes and classes as well as when she needs to do mailings to notify her customers about upcoming classes or special holiday sales. Her children are also learning a lot about business by helping Mom with simple tasks and she has hired another stay-at-home Mom to help with the decorating. Her home garden has become much larger as she has taken on more and more herb classes and now finds people wanting to buy herbs from her. And her small 10" herb gardens are selling like hotcakes!

Susan has been putting money away for her children's education as well as her retirement but she also has a savings account at her credit union. She only puts $20 a month into it but soon she will have the problem of figuring out who will take care of the business while she tours Europe for a month.

Charlie finds himself worrying about who to hire that he can depend on. And he knows he has got to put in a bigger parking lot. But he also knows that this type of worrying is much better than worrying about losing the farm. Yes, life is much busier than it was when he was just a farmer, but it is also more exciting and fun. And he is very happy to see his family so happy. Dickie, always the innovator, may still be just a teenager but he is talking with a couple of other dairymen about setting up a small cheese factory together for tourists. And Joan's idea of having an ice cream shop and store right on the road frontage road is looking very promising.

Helen is taking off next year from teaching. She went on one of her hiking trips and, as usual, had a few new people. One man did not impress her at all. He was about her age but very heavy. After all, she was out walking every morning and eating right and had lost her 60 pounds and looked great. In fact, this man, Larry, was very annoying. On the whole hike to the top of Mt. Diablo, he would not leave her alone. He just kept asking her questions. Well, she had to be polite. By the end of the day she knew he was determined to lose his extra weight, he loved the outdoors, worked as a computer programmer and loved reading mysteries and westerns. Then he asked her if she would be interested in having lunch with him tomorrow (Sunday).

'Thank goodness,' Helen thought. She was able to politely say that she would love to but attended church in the morning and had a couple of church meetings during the afternoon. She figured that was the end of it.

But Larry also knew how to be persistent. He called her one evening very late.

"Sorry to call so late but you seem to out each night. I was wondering if I could join your walking group."

"That would be fine but I live a good 15 miles from you."

"That's okay."

"And we meet very early, at 6:00 am."

"That's okay, too."

So now she would have to listen to him every morning! Monday morning Helen did not know how she was going to put up with him. Tuesday she thought he seemed to be talking and questioning her less. Wednesday he actually made her laugh. By Thursday she was thinking that maybe going to the movies with him would be okay. Six months later Larry proposed and Helen accepted.

He wasn't perfect but Helen had found someone who seemed to really care about and her feelings. They shared a lot of interests. In fact, he was a nice guy. Who says nice guys finish last?

So now Helen was taking off a year from teaching

to get ready for the new baby and have time to spend with him or her (they both liked surprises). Helen had seen her beliefs at work in her own life.

"Ask and you will receive.
Seek and you will find;
knock, and it will be opened to you."
Matthew 7:7

And Margie is still helping others build their dream lives.

"Make it so."
Capt. Picard of Star Trek: The Next Generation